Next Time They'll Come
to Count the Dead

Next Time They'll Come to Count the Dead

War and Survival in South Sudan

Nick Turse

Dispatch Books

Haymarket Books
Chicago, Illinois

Published in 2016 by
Haymarket Books
P.O. Box 180165
Chicago, IL 60618
773-583-7884
www.haymarketbooks.org
info@haymarketbooks.org

ISBN: 978-1-60846-648-1

Trade distribution:
In the US, Consortium Book Sales and Distribution, www.cbsd.com
In Canada, Publishers Group Canada, www.pgcbooks.ca
In the UK, Turnaround Publisher Services, www.turnaround-uk.com
All other countries, Publishers Group Worldwide, www.pgw.com

This book was published with the generous support of Lannan Foundation
and Wallace Action Fund.

Cover design by Eric Kerl. Cover image of a tank encountered on the side
of the road between Juba and Bor, South Sudan, February 26, 2015. Photo
by and courtesy of Nick Turse.

Printed in Canada by union labor.

Library of Congress Cataloging-in-Publication data is available.

1 3 5 7 9 10 8 6 4 2

Contents

A More Personal War

Their voices, sharp and angry, shook me from my slumber. I didn't know the language, but I instantly knew the translation. So I groped for the opening in the mosquito net, shuffled from my downy white bed to the window, threw back the stained tan curtain, and squinted into the light of a new day breaking in South Sudan. Below, in front of my guest house, one man was getting his ass kicked by another. A flurry of blows connected with his face and suddenly he was crumpled on the ground. Three or four men were watching.

The victor, still standing, appeared strong and confident. His sinewy arms seemed to have been carved from obsidian. Having won in decisive fashion, he turned his back and began walking away with a self-satisfied swagger. The other man staggered to his feet, his face contorted with a ragged, wounded-animal look—the one that seems to begin as an electric ache at the back of your jaw, drawing your lips back into a grimace as tears well up in your eyes. And what he did next seemed straight out of a movie. I couldn't believe I was seeing it.

The vast, rutted dirt field below me was filled with trash: half-burned water bottles, empty soda cans—and glass. And that furious man promptly did what I had previously only seen on screen. He grabbed a bottle by the neck—it might already have been broken or he might have shattered off the bottom with a quick rap on a rock—and in an instant he had himself an equalizer.

The ass-kicker spun around to find the tables turned and he knew it. The man with the bottle knew it, too. He was shouting and jabbing, though he wasn't actually close enough to do any damage. Nonetheless, with fear spreading across his face, the ass-kicker backpedaled, still talking loud but unmistakably in retreat.

It seemed clear enough that the man with the bottle didn't really have it in him to punch that jagged glass through the other's taut skin. His fury seemed to fade fast and he didn't press his advantage. Or maybe he was just afraid of what might happen if he were disarmed. Whatever the reason, cooler heads prevailed. The onlookers got him to drop his weapon and the combatants walked off in opposite directions. It was over, even if nothing else was in South Sudan.

At one point, as the two fought, I glanced back at the bed where my cell phone lay and nearly fetched it. The impulse to shoot a few pictures or some video footage of the unfolding scene was powerful and hardly surprising since I come from a culture now built around documenting and sharing even the most mundane happenings.

I didn't move, in part because I had no idea what was going on. If I recorded it, what then? What accompanying story could I tell? I knew that, short of one man killing the other, it was unlikely that anyone would be around by the time I threw on my clothes and got downstairs. Real-life fights rarely last long. And what, even if they spoke English, were these men going to tell me? Would I write about a personal skirmish over money or a woman or some drunken insult?

Thinking about it later, I came to see the episode as a metaphor for my situation. It was the summer of 2014 and the dawn of my first full day on my initial trip to South Sudan. I was there to get an on-the-ground look at a failing nation in the midst of a months-old civil war; a complex, partly tribal conflict that, in some ways, boiled down to a backyard fight between two men. And frankly, as with the morning struggle I had just witnessed, I had little idea of what was going on. Sure, I'd talked to humanitarian experts and South Sudanese in the United States. I'd read news articles and substantive reports by the United Nations, Human Rights Watch, and others. On the flight over, I'd finished a very good book on the country and a couple marginally useful ones before that, but I couldn't have been more of a neophyte standing there in the capital of a new nation, convulsed by a conflict that had already killed more than 10,000 people and left millions homeless or displaced.

Still, I came with a history that seemed suited to the situation. I'd spent parts of the previous decade wandering around post-conflict countries in Southeast Asia, unearthing evidence of horrendous crimes committed by the United States and its allies. I had traveled to remote Vietnamese villages no American had visited since my country's combat there ended in 1973, hamlets where the villagers might never have met an unarmed Westerner. I talked to people about rapes and murders and massacres, largely by American troops. I interviewed them about living for years under bombs and artillery shells and helicopter gunships that hunted humans from the sky. I spoke with women and men who saw their families cut down by American teenagers with automatic rifles. I talked with those who had lost limbs or eyes or were scorched by napalm or white phosphorous—incendiary weapons that melted faces or left the victims with imperfectly mended swaths of skin. And back in the United States, I spent endless hours with the men who had done these sorts of things to Vietnamese and Cambodians, as well as others who had refused to take part.

After more than 10 years immersed in atrocity, I needed a change so—obviously—I headed for a war zone filled with atrocities about which I knew next to nothing. But to me, it felt different. I wasn't about to repeat my work in Vietnam. I had landed in a place where history was being made and I was going to do my best to report on a different kind of war victim. This time, it was going to be displaced people trapped by the thousands on United Nations bases that had become almost like open-air prisons. It didn't take me long, of course, to realize that there was something unnervingly familiar about the work, about the grim tales I began to hear of suffering, privation, and loss (with women and children, as always, hit hardest). In talking to people in those sun-drenched limbos—refugees in their own country—it took next to no time for stories I recognized well to begin seeping into the interviews, tales of family members gunned down in the streets, of rapes and assaults, the sort of hideous acts that form the fabric of modern war, no matter what country, what area of the world.

I spent a couple weeks in-country talking to ordinary South Sudanese and humanitarian workers, taking stock as best I could—part of the time on the outskirts of Malakal, a war-ravaged town 515 kilometers north of Juba.

I traveled there, in the heart of the rainy season, to find a United Nations base drowning in a sea of muck and squalor. And I wiled away an evening with a couple of local journalists who had, in the wake of the war, signed on with the U.N. Bathed in an unnatural fluorescent glow, we talked shop after hours in their office. I wanted the inside story of South Sudan's crisis and they, in turn, wanted to know about me. Perhaps unsatisfied with my answers, one of them decided to consult Google for background. My book on the Vietnam War, *Kill Anything That Moves*, popped up instantly and he looked up from his monitor astonished. He had, after all, just told me about how a member of his family—a man of some standing—had apparently been the victim of a targeted killing in the opening salvo of the civil war. If I specialized in investigating crimes of war, the journalist wanted to know, why the hell wasn't I investigating war crimes in South Sudan? I came up with excuses, but my new acquaintance found them unconvincing and, in truth, I wasn't that convinced myself.

I spent that night on a cot in the back of a deserted office on that U.N. base thinking about what he had said and was still thinking about it the next day when I arrived at a nearby airport to catch a U.N. flight back to Juba. Of course, to call it an airport is a bit of a misnomer. By the time I arrived, it had devolved into an airstrip. Nobody seemed to use its vintage blue and white terminal building anymore. Instead, you drove past cold eyed Rwandan peacekeepers, U.N. troop trucks, and an armored personnel carrier or two, right up to the tarmac.

That's where I was when a large, nondescript white plane arrived. That in itself was hardly remarkable for Malakal. If it isn't a World Food Program flight, then it's a big-bellied plane hauling in supplies for some nongovernmental organization or a U.N. plane like the one that brought me there and would soon take me away.

This nondescript white plane, however, was different from the others. When the Canadair CRJ-100, with "Cemair" written across its tail, taxied up and its door opened, a group of young men in camouflage uniforms carrying assault rifles and machine guns emerged. And they were met there by scores of similarly attired, similarly armed young men who had arrived in a convoy just minutes before.

I'd never seen anything like it, so I pulled out my phone and tried to surreptitiously take a few photos. Not surreptitiously enough, it turned out. A commander spotted me and promptly headed my way, visibly angry and waving his finger "no." As I glanced to my left, a boy holding an AK-47 and following the officer's gaze turned toward me and with him came the barrel of his rifle.

I didn't think he was going to shoot me. There was no anger in his eyes. He didn't draw a bead on me. His finger may not even have been near the trigger. Still, he was a boy—he looked about 16—and he was holding an assault rifle and it was pointed in my direction, so I stepped lively to put the commander between him and me, while quickly shoving my phone in my pocket and apologizing profusely if not quite sincerely.

By the time my plane arrived and I was heading back to Juba, I was sure that I needed to return to South Sudan to talk to boys like that teenaged soldier; to spend more time on United Nations bases with people trapped in squalor; to try to understand how a new nation only years before "midwifed" by my own country and hailed as a great hope for Africa could be laid so low that people were starting to whisper "Rwanda" and talk about South Sudan as a possible next epicenter of genocide.

Even though I've spent considerably more time in the country since, I still don't claim to know much about this hot, land-locked, Texas-sized country, only a few years old, inhabited by 60 ethnic groups, and a population whose median age is 17.[1] But there are people who do know it intimately and I sought them out. For several weeks in early 2015, I spoke with U.N. officials and humanitarian workers, military officers and child soldiers, politicos and "big men," but mostly with ordinary people whose already tragedy-tinged lives had been blown apart by a violent power struggle that began on a military base in Juba and spread like a pandemic into the neighboring streets, then through the capital, and finally into rural hot zones to the north.

No one knows how many men, women, and children were slaughtered in Juba's streets that first night, December 15, 2013, or how many died in the following weeks as war flared in the towns of Bentiu, Malakal, and Bor, or in the spasms of violence elsewhere in the months that followed. Nobody knows where all the bodies went; where all the mass graves are located. But when so many die, others in similar situations do survive and I sat down with scores of them in plastic-tarp shanties, dimly lit bars, deserted workplaces after hours, or under the welcome shade of sun-scalded trees, or we spoke by phone or on Skype in Africa and the United States. With a vividness that often astounded me, they described their stories of hardship and horror and some-times even told me of small victories.

There is a chance that by the time this book is published a peace deal signed as the manuscript was being completed will take root—unlike the many ceasefires before it that shattered, some within hours—and that the world's newest nation will be on a path to reconciliation and prosperity; a chance, that is, that the promise of that country's Independence Day in 2011 will fi-nally be realized.[2] There is also the potential for so much worse, the possibility that recent reports of government forces raping girls and burning them alive, castrating young boys and allowing them to bleed out, or crushing people with armored vehicles are a prelude to an even more brutal, sadistic spree of violence on an even more massive scale, a chance that "Rwanda" could become a reality in South Sudan in the months or years to come.

Whatever happens to the country and its long-suffering people, the voices in this book serve, I hope, as a testament both to the struggles and the courage of the victims of violence there and as a cautionary tale of the sort of chaos and mayhem that may lie ahead.

Next Time They'll Come to Count the Dead: War and Survival in South Sudan

It's dark and hot and he selects a quiet spot beyond the edge of the patio. Under the wispy branches of a mimosa tree in a desiccated dirtscape near the gated, guarded parking lot, we sit at a table for eight, just the two of us. The waiter is upon us immediately. I order a Tusker beer. My companion, water. With the dim golden glow of patio lights at our feet, I make small talk until the tall, young server is out of earshot. It wasn't easy to schedule this meeting and we're already an hour late, so I get down to it immediately.

Some nights, this is a sweaty expat scene packed with Americans, Canadians, and Europeans. Thursdays, it's devoted to salsa dancing and late Sundays into early Mondays, it's light on people but heavy on sound—the throbbing, thumping bass of African and American beats spun by the DJ at the club next door. Tonight, though, it's sleepy, hushed, half-deserted—a scene befitting a bar named for a dead dog. Still, I automatically fall silent whenever a couple straggles by or our server checks my progress on the beer and my source's plastic bottle of Aqua'na.

Maybe for my benefit, maybe to satisfy the hovering waiter, my table-mate orders a beer, too. As he does, the sheen on his skin—it was around 97 degrees at sunset and must still be in the low 90s—allows me to take note of his features even in the darkness. Rawboned with taut skin, his cheeks are slightly sunken, his face clean-shaven. His head is shaved too. A vein on its left side bulges. It's hard not to look at it. His eyes are serious, but there's a spark to them. They narrow whenever he's making a point and he has many to make.

The waiter comes back with a Tusker Lite, seems satisfied, and finally leaves us be. It's then that the grim subjects automatically come up. He speaks in a blur of words, racing through one nightmarish point after another. By the time I've deciphered one sentence, he's leapfrogged two ahead. We talk about war, murder, and accountability, but there's really only one question I want answered this night and it's been on my mind for months.

My drinking companion is leaving the country tomorrow and the hour is getting late. With a final glance to my blindside and then the parking lot, I lean in and ask Edmund Yakani if he knows where the bodies are. All those people must be somewhere, I say. So where are the mass graves?[1]

◆

South Sudan is the youngest country in the world, tucked beneath its former parent nation with whom it shares half its name. It's sandwiched between the Central African Republic, the Democratic Republic of Congo, Uganda, Kenya, and Ethiopia. When independence came in 2011, there was a lot of hope here. So much, in fact, that it seemed as if old wounds from 1989 and 1991 and 1993 and the rest of almost five decades of civil war might be swept away in a tide of ecstatic liberation—joy on the streets of

Juba, the capital, forgiveness in towns from Bentiu to Bor, Wardak to Wau. But before long the old fissures, the old wounds, began to resurface—jagged memories that refused to stay buried, saw-toothed truths that tore at the fabric of the nation. "Blood will have blood," wrote William Shakespeare and it didn't take long before the words of the greatest playwright of southern Sudan's former colonial overlord started to come true; the sins of the fathers became the terrors of the sons. But it was rarely the *right* sons—if there could ever be *right* sons. And all too often it was the daughters and their children, sometimes even babies.

In December 2013, months of tension between President Salva Kiir, a Dinka—that is, a member of the the largest tribe in the country—and Riek Machar, his vice president and a Nuer—a member of the second largest tribe—whom he had dismissed months before, reached a boiling point.[2] On the night of the 15th, fighting broke out in the headquarters barracks of the army in the capital, Juba, between Dinka and Nuer members of the Presidential Guard, also known as the "Tiger Division."[3]

Simon Wuor had a front-row seat as the violence unfolded and later told me his story. His home in Juba's Khor William neighborhood was across the road from the sprawling military compound known as General Headquarters (GHQ) or Giyada. Around 10:15 p.m., he turned off the nightly news on SSTV, the national channel, and retired to his bedroom. It wasn't long before he heard the pop, pop, pop. Three shots. Then more. Then, a continuous rattle of automatic weapons. He'd heard gunfire from headquarters before, many times in fact. But never like this.

Wuor, like most of his neighbors, assumed that whatever battle was going on among the soldiers of the Tiger Division would remain confined to the base. Strife and South Sudan go together. The country has been engulfed in violence for decades, since long before independence. Armed men did what armed men have long been wont to do. Wuor took it for granted that, whatever was going on, it would end quickly.

It didn't.

Within minutes, news of the fighting was pinging from one cell phone to another in the capital and, before long, out in the countryside, too. A friend stationed at the GHQ across the street called to say that a firefight had broken out when Dinka soldiers tried to disarm their Nuer comrades so they could arrest senior officials from that tribe. He told Wuor to hunker down and stay indoors. The 27-year-old local supervisor for an international nongovernmental organization (NGO), his wife, and three children, ages six, three-and-a-half, and two, huddled under a bed, as bullets ripped through their corrugated metal home.

The gunfire was constant until about 1 a.m. when it softened, as Wuor recalls, before it broke back into a rattling roar. It kept up until dawn. Peeking outside, he saw soldiers swarming through the streets. So the family locked themselves in until the afternoon. By 3 p.m., the gunfire had quieted down and Wuor spoke with neighbors who were weighing a plan to make a run for Jebel Checkpoint, a neighborhood where there was said to be little fighting. It was on the way to "U.N. House"—the colloquial name for one of the two bases in Juba of the United Nations Mission in South Sudan (UNMISS)—a place of potential safety. A group of women and children were about to set off on the long trek there and, after brief consideration, Wuor decided to send his wife and children with them. He was planning to stay put to protect his home from looters. He could always run if things got worse.

They did.

At 4:30, Wuor's phone rang again. You need to leave now, his friend told him. The Dinka Presidential Guard is on a killing spree, searching house to house. Take any route you think is safe. Just get away.

Simon Wuor isn't a big man. The first time we spoke, he was wearing a plaid button-down shirt slightly too large for his modest frame, olive-drab pants, and red flip-flops. Wiry, with close-cropped hair, prominent cheekbones, and chin stubble that fades along the jaw line, there's a nervous energy to him. He makes quick, staccato gestures, jabbing at the air or floor with his index finger to emphasize points. He's a Nuer, and so the potential target, as his friend informed him, of the fury of the Dinka troops. He had, however, one thing in his favor. He does not sport the traditional tribal markings—ridge-like scars across the forehead, known as *gaar*—that identify men as Nuer and so, that December night, marked them for death.

Grabbing a black backpack and tossing in whatever crucial documents were at hand—his school diplomas as well as education certificates for secretarial skills and computer science—he began walking toward the University of Juba, in the vague hope that it might be safe.

As would happen again and again over the hours to come, Wuor was stopped by Dinka troops from the Sudan People's Liberation Army (SPLA) who had set up impromptu checkpoints across the city. And here was where his other great advantage came into play.[4] All over Juba, Dinka forces were employing words as weapons. Sometimes, they called out to people in the Nuer language. Respond in kind and you were shot.[5] Other times, they used their own tongue to similar effect. "They greeted us in Dinka language," a student recalled, "when we failed to answer they said that means you are Nuer and we are looking for Nuer." The student managed to escape his residential compound, but four of his companions didn't. He returned to find them all dead.[6]

Tipped off to the ethnic nature of the budding bloodbath, Wuor responded to questions in Arabic and English. Suspicious about his backpack, the soldiers would glance inside, see no weapons, and send him on his way. This happened again and again, and not once was he asked for the national ID in his pocket which identifies him as originally from Leer County in Unity State, a place that would instantly brand him a Nuer. From one roadblock to another he walked, sometimes at a brisk pace, without ever letting himself break into a run.

Then he saw them.

Up ahead, two of his cousins had been stopped at a checkpoint. Seated on the ground, they were being viciously beaten by Dinka soldiers. They were cringing and wincing as rifle butts slammed into their heads, their faces contorted in pain. Wuor's eyes met theirs and a moment of recognition flashed between them. He quickly adjusted his gaze, looked away, and pretended not to know them. "It hurt me in my heart," he says, his voice cracking as he recalls that moment. "It was so difficult."

Leaving them to their fate, he threaded his way through the streets, falling in with a group of Ugandan nationals for a while.[7] All of them were by then headed for the UNMISS compound known as Tomping, before he suddenly turned toward U.N. House on the other side of town, the direction he knew his wife and children had taken.

Wuor saw the bodies of soldiers and civilians in the streets everywhere he went. He had had to step over one just to leave his own front gate. And everywhere, he saw fellow Nuers being detained, but he swore to me that he wasn't scared. I responded incredulously. How could that be possible? He didn't have time for it, was his reply. He was fixated on getting somewhere, anywhere safe. All his thoughts, all his energies were focused on that goal as he ping-ponged through the capital. That only changed when he made it to Yei Road, the final leg of the journey to U.N. House.

Near a fork in that road known as Eye Radio junction, he came upon a scene that, even amid the carnage of that night, staggered him. There were bodies, blood-soaked and bullet-ridden, lining the sides of the dirt track. "They were civilians of every type. Men, women, and children," he recalled. "That's when the fear set in for me." More corpses than he had seen all evening—and here on the road that he knew his wife and children had taken. "I was so frightened." Wuor tells me that he couldn't bring himself to look closely. He didn't want to see his family murdered and left to rot at this desolate crossroads. He's uncertain just how many bodies were there. "Many," is all he can say.

Multiple witnesses recall seeing Dinka soldiers holding about 20 Nuer men, captured while attempting to flee to U.N. House, in a shelter not far from the crossroads. They watched as three of the Nuers were separated from the rest and shot dead. Another man detained near that road junction reported seeing the corpses of five men there.[8] A Nuer man who asked that I refer to him only as Thudan, his first name, tells me that he also traveled down Yei Road sometime after Wuor. "There were a lot of bodies there. Not only men, but also women and children," he says. "I regretted taking that route. If I had known what I'd see, I'd never have gone that way."[9]

Witnesses also reported seeing very near U.N. House the bodies of three men who had been murdered. A woman told Human Rights Watch that her husband, a civilian, was killed at a military checkpoint near the U.N. base.[10] Gatthuoy Gatkoi, a 31-year-old man whose tribal marks have left him with angry-looking, perpetually knitted brows, assures me that he saw many bodies on Yei Road between the junction and the UNMISS base, including two men he knew. "That's when I became gripped with fear. That's when I started running."[11]

Head out to Yei Road on the outskirts of the capital today and you'll find busted tarmac in some spots, gravel in others, everything gradually dissolving into cocoa-colored, heavily rutted, undulating earth. U.N. road crews are forever filling in runnels, rolling areas flat, trying to keep the road passable, but it's a losing battle.

Keep on bumping along beyond the rusting, slightly askew billboard that advertises a gated community called, I kid you not, Liberation Estates ("Villas to Let") and sooner or later you'll find the spot where Simon Wuor and others say that so many were killed.

Visit Eye Radio junction—that intersection where two dirt tracks split off from the main road, one heading for a radio station (98.6 on the dial) whose tagline is "Your Eye on South Sudan"—and you'll find no evidence of the moment in December 2013 when it became a killing ground. There is no monument to the dead or memorial of any sort. Instead, Toyota SUVs, lumbering water trucks, and oil tankers kick up clouds of dust and the men who drive the motorbikes (called "boda-bodas") that serve as taxis stop here at ramshackle shops selling cheap drinks and snacks.

Drive past the junction, bearing right, past mud brick huts, traditional waddle-and-daub, thatched-roof *tukuls,* and corrugated roof shanties, past a business catering to an increasingly connected world (God Knows Cell Phone Charging), while to your right the land rises into rolling hills of chocolate-brown granite and hardy green scrub. Then, hang a left and head down a corridor of shacks and shanties, the S.M. Wine "Galary"—a metal hut that offers liquor and cigarettes—the Chelsea Hall Restaurant, which attracts a late afternoon crowd, the Florida Inn, a barber shop called "Salon of All Nations," as well as a bevy of homespun businesses selling cell phone minutes, soda, packaged snacks, pineapples, bananas, and oranges, and you finally arrive at the main gate of U.N. House, just as Simon Wuor did on the night of December 16, 2013, just as his family had hours earlier. They were reunited at the base and they haven't left since.

Over the course of December 16, renegade Nuer troops fought rear-guard actions as they were pushed out of Juba by determined soldiers from various government forces. That afternoon, Salva Kiir—rarely seen without the black cowboy hat given to him by U.S. president George W. Bush or the replacement provided by Secretary of State John Kerry—appeared on television clad in tiger-stripe camouflage and announced that his troops had full control of the capital. Kiir said nothing about the attacks on Nuers, nor did he call for the protection of Nuer civilians, even as thousands of them were pouring into the two UNMISS bases to escape violence and death in the streets.[12]

By then, government forces were conducting house-to-house searches throughout Juba—in Jebel in the southwest, Munuki just to its north, Mangaten and New Site yet further north, Mia Saba in the northeast, Lologo and Khor William near the GHQ, and Gudele in the east; they were, that is, looting homes, rounding up military-age Nuer men wherever they could find them, and sometimes killing them.[13]

Sheldon Wardwell isn't a Nuer or a Dinka. He isn't even South Sudanese. A self-proclaimed "long-haired white kid" with blond locks somewhere on the continuum between surfer and hippie, this 27-year-old native Californian arrived in Juba on December 11 to begin a stint with Nonviolent Peaceforce or NP, an NGO that provides a "protective presence" for civilians in crisis zones. Little more than a skeleton crew was there holding things together over the holidays.

Wardwell had worked in South Sudan before in fairly austere conditions. "I thought it was pretty extreme," he confides, but it would prove to be nothing compared to what lay ahead.

He spent the entire night of the 15th in a compound near the U.N. base at Tomping, watching tracer fire streak this way and that. With dawn, the rattle of battle began to die down, so he headed for his room to finally get some sleep. No sooner had he stripped down to his boxer shorts than he heard a loud bang followed by shouting. Out the window he saw 10 or 12 young men, some in military uniforms, some in civilian clothes. Most had AK-47s. One carried a bow and arrow.

Dinka soldiers from the SPLA, they were screaming at Wardeell's team leader, an inexperienced executive from the home office covering for vacationing staff who knew little about South Sudan. "Where's the other white man?!" they kept demanding. Wardwell remembers stepping back and sitting down on his bed, legs crossed Indian-style, to process the situation. He ran through a range of scenarios: the door was unlocked so they might just barge right in; or, if I don't come out, they might shoot through the door; or they might start busting into other rooms housing the local staff—men and women—and a young German volunteer. Feeling especially exposed in his underwear, Wardwell quickly pulled on some clothes, opened his door, threw up his hands, and stepped into a scene that sounds right out of the movies. An email he sent a friend later that day read, in part: "I had to come out of the room. . . Five days in-country and I've already had an AK-47 to the head. Most importantly, we're all okay and determined. But they did steal everything of mine of value, including my laptop with my Final Paper for Professor Kammen. Dave, please update him it's going to be late."[14]

"Two goddamn papers, all that work," Wardwell recalls, thinking of graduate school assignments he had just finished. He watched a soldier walk off with his computer, while another took his Samsung Galaxy phone. "All my contacts are in that. How am I going to call my mom?" he remembers thinking. The glowering young men kept their rifles trained on him. One of them, visibly drunk, seemed to delight in making the aid workers cower. Still, the Dinka soldiers seemed unwilling to press their luck, even with the city in chaos. After 10 minutes, they walked out of the compound with laptops, phones, and any other communications gear they could find, and that was that.[15]

Though Wardwell and his team leader were unharmed, at least two international aid workers—one from Solidarités International, the other from International Medical Corps—were killed elsewhere during the first two weeks of fighting.[16] For South Sudanese, of course, the toll was so much worse. Human Rights Watch received more than 60 reports of killings in Juba alone during December. The United Nations chronicled hundreds of deaths. The South Sudan Human Rights Commission, a government agency that monitors human rights but has no prosecutorial powers, reported that "between 16th and 18th December over 600 people mainly Nuer ethnic group were killed and more than 800 wounded in Juba and its suburbs."[17] Some Nuers claim that 20,000 or more of their brethren were slaughtered in Juba—a number that seems absurdly high.[18] The truth is, however, that no one knows how many died, nor will anyone… ever.

South Sudan's government launched at least three major investigations into human rights abuses during the Juba crisis in early 2014—by the police, the military, and a group headed by a former chief justice of the Supreme Court of South Sudan. All have been shadowed in secrecy. All issued reports that were never made public. An ex officio investigation by the Ministry of Justice has seemingly vanished as well, if it ever existed at all.

The government of South Sudan nonetheless claims it has effective mechanisms for military justice and holds people accountable for crimes against civilians. Is there any evidence for this? "No," says Ibrahim Wani, director of the Human Rights Division of the UNMISS, representative of the High Commissioner for Human Rights, and former dean and chief advisor at the U.S. Department of Defense's Africa Center for Strategic Studies. "We've been told investigations are being conducted, formal bodies have been established for that purpose, and in some cases outcomes have been reached, but those outcomes were not shared."[19]

South Sudan's Human Rights Commission did make an effort to observe, monitor, and collect information in the wake of the crisis, but never launched actual investigations despite its legal mandate to do so. "We're in a very tricky situation," says Victor Lado Caesar, executive director of the commission. "Some people in the government might not be happy with this work."

Tall, straight-spined, and dark-eyed, Caesar claims that it's been extremely difficult to gather evidence. In addition, although South Sudan's legal code—section 39, subsection 2 of the Southern Sudan Human Rights Act of 2009, for those keeping score—mandates that other investigatory bodies must "immediately provide information" to his commission about suspected human rights violations, its officials were refused access to the report by the former chief justice. "When peace comes, maybe then we can finally start investigating," Caesar adds with resignation.[20] This is a constant refrain I hear from South Sudanese and a sorry kind of confirmation that there will be little hope of justice in the near future.

In 2014, Kiir's government and Machar's rebels repeatedly engaged in talks that resulted in one ceasefire after another, each of which collapsed almost immediately. While I was in South Sudan, another potential power-sharing agreement to bring Machar back into the fold was announced and once again any exploration of accountability was tabled in the name of stability. Of course, that agreement imploded, too.

In February 2014, South Sudan's government announced the arrest of about 100 of its soldiers apparently implicated in targeted killings, but would not provide information on the nature of the investigation, the identities of the accused, or the charges against them. The next month, the government claimed that all those men had somehow escaped during clashes, over salary payments, between members of the military.[21] I ask the SPLA's judge advocate general and director of military justice about the incident and he responds in the vaguest, briefest possible way. "There was heavy fighting," he says, "so everybody escaped."

"Every single one of them? All 100?" I ask with skepticism.

"Yes," he replies, his deadpan face giving away nothing. End of discussion. According to a U.N. official I later spoke with, the government also claimed that a fire had conveniently destroyed the records relating to the escapees and that, as a result, the cases had been abandoned.[22] Another senior U.N. official, confirming that the government was standing by this absurd story, added, "These guys are good. The South Sudanese are quite adept at the art of delay."[23]

I mention all of this to Caesar and he tells me that the arrests, when announced, had given him hope. "We asked to visit them, but then the government told us that all of them escaped. We asked them why they didn't publish their names, provide further information about the allegations against them, send their pictures to the borders so they couldn't escape. But they did nothing. This led us to conclude…" But he trails off before finishing the thought. It's too absurd. Instead, he breaks into laughter and then confirms that none of the men have ever been located or re-arrested, pointing out another curiosity: "In all that heavy fighting, all those men, not one of those 100 were killed." He then turns solemn and leans across his desk, his eyes locking in on mine. "This is a very big problem," he confides, his voice dropping, "this impunity."

Investigations may vanish, men may disappear, and records go up in smoke, but in South Sudan you don't have to search very hard or go very far to find information about such crimes. It's the corroboration that's the difficult part, with all sides in the conflict having their own compelling reasons for inventing, embellishing, ignoring, or obscuring the events being discussed. I wile away hours speaking to people whose stories seem too perfect or too murky, too contrived or too difficult to possibly confirm. I irritate people by asking questions they've already answered, pick at weak spots in stories, seize upon possible inconsistencies, fret over whether the trouble could lie in the translation from Dinka or Nuer or Murle or accented English that sounds broken and foreign to my ear or if it's the narrative itself that's at fault.

I'm told of soldiers forcing civilians to eat human flesh or drink human blood. I dismiss the lurid accounts at first, until I hear them too many times from too many sources. I listen to stories of mass rapes and mutilations and men and women set aflame. I hear about horrific sexual assaults and other acts of shocking cruelty. People tell me names of those killed in the violence and I check them against the few fragmentary lists available, against reports issued by the United Nations, Human Rights Watch, and Médecins Sans Frontières (Doctors Without

Borders), but it's generally a fruitless exercise since the victims of most of these recent horrors remain unrecorded.

Roda Nyajiech Juch—a substantial woman in a white and purple cotton dress with a simple gold band snug on her left ring finger—can't stop wringing her hands as she tells me, for example, about eight students killed near Juba's Jebel Checkpoint: Kuong Gatpan, Puok Thichot, Kam Machak, Puok Wiech, Leklek Kai, and three brothers, Kai Thoan, Gatkoi Thoan, and Dak Thoan.[24] I can't find their names in any report or list, which doesn't mean that they didn't die exactly as she tells me they did. More than a year after the crisis began, some people are just now coming forward to report nightmarish atrocities in places where the United Nation had no access, says the U.N.'s Wani. Even his organization, which has issued some of the most detailed reports on crimes in this period, still considers cases from the early days of the war to be open and incomplete.

"Given the context in which we work," says the Ugandan who was once a law professor at the Universities of Virginia and Missouri, "you really can't bring closure to it. We're not even working in a context such as when you're pursuing a prosecution and you can therefore say, 'I've gained all the information that I need and I'll move forward'.... By definition, our work has been preliminary in the sense that if we receive any allegations of human rights violations occurring, we try as much as possible to talk to witnesses. We try to corroborate the statements that we gather from witnesses, either by site visits or other interviews. To the extent possible, we try to talk to people who might be implicated in those violations.

"Oftentimes," he continues, "it's not very easy in the context of a human rights investigation. In many, many instances, it's not like investigating a crime scene, where you have firsthand witnesses, you have access to the crime scene itself, you have access to weapons, you can do various scientific analyses, you have the power to subpoena witnesses. We don't have any of that, so in many instances when you have problems of human rights violations, it's very confusing, very murky, especially when people are on the run. What that all means is that you're constantly trying to substantiate whatever information you have. We make a threshold determination when we reach that point that we're sufficiently persuaded that something may have happened."

In his orderly office in Juba that afternoon in February—the month the Nuers call "Fire"—Wani wears a white button-down shirt with olive pants that are as nondescript as his brown slip-on shoes. Quick on the draw with his air conditioner's remote control, he adjusts it incessantly. At one point, I wonder if he wants to sweat me out, but I keep the questions coming and he continues to answer in his measured, precise way.

I ask Wani if his investigators have been collecting forensic evidence, photographs, and video footage to build cases for future prosecutions. No, he answers, they have almost exclusively been gathering testimony and issuing reports.

That hasn't sat well with some. "The Human Rights Division likes to be sensational," a senior United Nations official tells me, "but they don't appear to like to do the hard work like the preservation of evidence and that is something that has really pissed me off about [the] Human Rights [Division] and the international community, in general. They have not really been serious about the preservation of evidence for courts… [The] Human Rights [Division people] are going out there and investigating crimes against humanity and human rights abuses, but they are reduced to taking conversation notes. That is not admissible in any court of law and, in fact, no human rights person can appear in a court of law to give evidence in the first place."

Despite a plethora of trained policemen from all over the world and more than 100 lawyers at hand, he says none of these U.N. professionals were utilized to preserve evidence. "So sure, they've done the surface skimming. They've got numbers and names, but they don't have testimony taken under oath. Who should be doing that job? People who have the right to appear in court. So the United Nations should have immediately launched training programs for South Sudanese civil society lawyers to take statements because they can appear in court." He explains that gathering proper evidence would have been as simple as having South Sudanese videotaping testimony of witnesses to the atrocities.[25]

There's certainly no shortage of potential witnesses to interview. I locate a native of Unity State in the north of the country who arrived in Juba in late 2013 to look for work as a nurse. He's been trapped on a U.N. base for more than a year and fears giving his name. The night of December 15, staying with relatives near Jebel Checkpoint, he began to hear gunfire. Like Simon Wuor, he assumed it was a battle between soldiers that wouldn't spread, but when the clatter of automatic weapons kept up, he peered into the darkness and saw flashes of gunfire light up the night.

By the early morning, he tells me, Presidential Guard troops were in his neighborhood, shooting randomly. He and his housemates sat tight, not knowing what to do. When a military vehicle rolled up to the traditional grass structure that could easily have been flattened, the men began filing out. The first two to exit, his cousin and an in-law tried to tell the soldiers that they were civilians and had nothing to do with the fighting. The nurse watched as a soldier pointed his AK-47 at each of them. "The Tiger soldier shot them," he says. Two of his other companions made a break for it and were gunned down.

The rest of the men were lined up. The soldiers told them to make up a song about the Nuer being chased out of Juba and sing it in Dinka, a language they didn't know. Failing their task, the men were packed into the bed of a large truck with up to 200 other prisoners.

"We have a saying: 'Death and life are linked together,'" he tells me. "I had no idea if I would survive." The truck rumbled down a road leading toward a wasteland behind U.N. House. He was by then convinced they were being taken to a secluded killing ground. Suddenly, a man in a military uniform, a major with military intelligence, halted the truck. They couldn't make out what he was telling the driver—he spoke in Arabic—but as the truck turned around, he climbed into the back with them. Soon, they arrived at the military intelligence compound at general headquarters. The major assigned guards to watch over the men through the night. From a distance, they saw UNMISS vehicles arrive and U.N. personnel head into the military intelligence facility. The UNMISS officials left and returned three more times. According to my interviewee, the 200 prisoners spent the night at the facility and the next day, instead of being killed were loaded onto a truck and received a military escort to the gate of U.N. House. He has lived there ever since.[26]

Not all men rounded up by government forces were so fortunate. The Gudele neighborhood in western Juba became an epicenter of atrocity. During the night of the 15th and into the next day, soldiers and policemen roamed the area, yanking Nuer men from cars, detaining them at checkpoints, and marching them at gunpoint from their homes to the so-called Police Building, a base for joint units of policemen, army troops, and other security forces created in 2012 to tackle rampant crime in the capital. The United Nations and human rights groups say that hundreds of

Nuer men were brought to the compound and locked in a stiflingly hot room. Several of them apparently died from overheating or by suffocation in that crowd of prisoners. Survivors said they saw or heard men being shot outside the room—a prelude to what occurred after sundown.[27]

At around 8 p.m., troops began firing AK-47 assault rifles and PKM machine guns through the windows, riddling the men inside with bullets. Many collapsed, gasping, screaming, bleeding. "The room was very bright with bullets," said a survivor.[28] The few who lived to tell of the horror did so only because the dead fell on top of them, shielding them from the bullets and then from discovery by troops who canvased the room, executing the injured. Some spent the night and a large part of the next day huddled among the corpses. "It was horrible, because to survive I had to cover myself with the bodies of dead people... the bodies started to smell really bad," one of them told the *Guardian*.[29]

As is true with most mass killings, fixing a number to this slaughter remains an exercise in uncertainty. Some estimates topped out around 200. Ivan Simonovic, the United Nations' assistant secretary-general for human rights, offered an estimate of 200 to 300 dead.[30] A U.N. report claimed "at least 300."[31] Human Rights Watch suggested that the number could be as high as 400.[32] Felix Taban, on the other hand, couldn't be more precise. The dead, he said, numbered 386. I ask him how he can be so sure of that number and he replies that it was the "official count."

Taban, a Muru hailing from the country's Western Equatoria state, and an officer with the National Security Service, was dispatched to the Gudele area with two platoons of Presidential Guards and National Security Service troops under his command. He sent one unit to a neighborhood known as Gudele 1. The other he accompanied to Gudele Center. What he found there was evidence of a bloodbath on the level of Wounded Knee, Lidice, My Lai, or El Calabozo.

The area was deserted by the time he arrived. No other soldiers. No civilians. No gunfire. No movement. Just shell casings. And flies. And bodies.

Corpses lay all around the Police Building in ones and twos, but inside it was a reeking, bloody killing ground. "I was completely shocked to see it," Taban confesses. "I realized then that I needed to leave this government." I ask to see evidence that he is who he says he is, that he really did work for the secret police. He produces a government photo ID: Felix Taban, National Security Service, Internal Security Bureau.

A bullet-shaped man with a broad face and a shaved head, even in a polo shirt and slacks Taban projects an air of military authority. He claims that what he did next was telephone Major General Marial Chanuong Yol Mangok, commander of the Presidential Guard, to report the mass of corpses, clothes soaked in blood, bodies already beginning to bloat in the heat.[33] Mangok—since named to a U.S. sanctions list for, according to Secretary of State Kerry, "violent attacks against civilians in Juba"—expressed neither outrage nor horror.[34] He didn't ask questions or demand answers. Instead he dispatched four large trucks and five or six military personnel clad in white smocks. They were the ones who gave Taban that figure, 386. (They also paid some of Taban's men to help them clean out the Police building with water and brooms.) Those smocked military personnel then proceeded to fill all four vehicles with bodies and, when the trucks pulled away with their ghastly cargo, there were still bodies left in that room. Where the trucks went, Taban didn't know. But when they returned, they were empty and the process began all over again— another four trucks' worth.[35]

Sheldon Wardwell, the American aid worker held at gunpoint, never saw trucks laden with bodies, but he heard about them. In those chaotic days, a hardy band of NGO workers regrouped at the U.N.'s Tomping base and teamed up to provide services to ever more frightened, desperate people. It was a moment when many expat humanitarians were leaving South Sudan in a hurry. Wardwell was determined to stay. "I personally felt that this was the time to be there," he says.

Wardwell joined a team of about eight protection workers, the first group of internationals to head back into Juba. They had no weapons, flak jackets, or armored vehicles, nothing but moral force and the faith that their presence alone might save lives. In a two-car convoy, they drove into hard-hit areas like Gudele and Jebel and watched as looters cleaned out Nuer homes. "Whole sections of neighborhoods were abandoned. In some areas, it was like going into a ghost town," Wardwell remembers. A ghost town with angry guards at checkpoints like those Simon Wuor had navigated through.

Ibrahim Wani tells me that his U.N. coworkers venturing into these same neighborhoods, encountered knots of menacing government troops. "Some of my colleagues had to run," he acknowledges. "Somebody comes at you with very aggressive questioning: 'What are you doing here? What's your purpose?' We had people turned back from places."

Jehanne Henry of Human Rights Watch had such an experience when trying to investigate the Police Building at Gudele. "I was accosted by an angry drunk soldier and nearly arrested by another group of soldiers," she wrote afterward. "After spotting yet another group of soldiers at the gate, we turned around."[36]

For days, Wardwell's tiny team mapped out the safest routes to travel and developed plans for what to do if shooting broke out before beginning to crisscross the city, facing down AK-47s in the hands of grim-faced soldiers, while they searched for dead bodies and the most vulnerable of the living. I ask Wardwell if they actually rescued anyone and he seems hesitant to answer. So I prod and finally, reluctantly he tells me that, yes, a number of times they found persons in fear of their lives, ushered them into their car, made them lie down out of sight, and then drove them to a safe area.

When I press for more, he tells me of a time when they received a call from an international compound—he won't say which one. A local man, completely naked, had scaled two walls, climbing over barbed wire, and snuck into its kitchen. He'd been hiding there for two days, thoroughly petrified. He had since been clothed, but wouldn't leave and no one would agree to come get him. In those chaotic days, aid workers often did things that in ordinary times would have been inconceivable, especially for a young, low-level NGO staffer. Wardwell tells me that he grabbed a vehicle, drove out on his own, and brought the man back to the U.N. base himself. That, I tell him, was a gutsy move, but he shakes off the flattery. "It took a lot of dedication," I add, and without responding, he lets the comment stand.

There were bodies lying out in the street, Wardwell recalls, but—about a week after the fighting started—no heaps of corpses in Juba. "I was actually shocked at how few bodies we found," he says. What there was plenty of, he and others assure me, was evidence that large numbers of people had been killed: blood on the ground, blood in homes, the sickening smell of corpses, tens of thousands of frightened refugees flooding into U.N. protection sites, the testimony of locals who told of Nuer neighbors being executed. "The first body I saw was a man whose hands were still tied behind his back, who had been shot through the head."

I ask Wardwell to sum up just what those days were like. "It was a head fuck," he replies and promptly apologizes for his language. I tell him it sounds like an apt description. "It was very scary. It was surreal. I remember very specifically thinking that I had just spent Christmas Day driving around looking for dead bodies, looking for mass graves."[37]

◆

South Sudan is no stranger to mass graves, mass killings, massacres. *Fire and Sword in the Sudan*, an 1896 memoir by Rudolf Slatin, an Austrian military officer who served in the region, recounts the treatment of two different southern Sudanese peoples by their Arab neighbors to the north:

> Zeki's forces had dispersed all the Shilluk gathering through-
> out the country, and destroyed their villages… the Khalifa
> [then] ordered him… to raid the Dinka tribe, who had already
> made their submission without fighting, seize their cattle and
> enslave their wives and children. These unsuspecting Blacks
> were summoned together under the pretext of a great feast;
> and when all had assembled, they were massacred almost to a
> man, and their wives, children, and cattle carried off.[38]

Slatin's memoir and others like it detail a time of great suffering marked by brutal extermination campaigns, massacres, slavery, and famine. Up to 5 million Sudanese reportedly died during this Victorian-age holocaust.[39]

There are also ancient enmities among the peoples of South Sudan, including centuries-old antagonisms between the Dinka and Nuer, not to mention hostilities among other ethnic groups, as well as intra-tribal clan conflicts.[40] The abduction of women and children and cattle raids have long been a feature of life in rural areas. A civil war between the Sudanese government and southern rebels—commonly portrayed as a battle of North versus South, Arabs versus Africans, Muslims versus Christians and pagans, lighter- versus darker-skinned people—raged from 1955 to 1972, ending with the granting of greater autonomy to southern Sudan.

In 1983, Sudan's president lit a tinderbox of growing tensions. He attempted a land grab to cheat southerners out of a wealth of oil discovered in their territory and followed that with a decision to introduce sharia law. A second civil war soon erupted. For more than 20 years, the Sudan People's Liberation Movement and its rebel army, the SPLA—with Salva Kiir and Riek Machar in high posts under the command of an American-educated Sudanese military officer, John Garang—fought a brutal independence struggle against Sudan, marked by shifting alliances and tangled factionalism.

These two civil wars were typified by tremendous suffering and death. The first cost 500,000 lives.[41] The second left more than 2 million dead of violence, starvation, and disease, and another 4 million displaced.[42] A famine in Ethiopia in the mid-1980s galvanized the world's attention, searing images of unimaginable misery into the minds of a generation. Perhaps the worst of it was seen at a camp in the town of Korem. An aid worker told the BBC that it was "the closest thing to hell on earth."[43] And yet, hardly noticed by much of the world, the death rates in Sudan were reportedly higher.[44] In addition to hunger, the fighting was ferocious and atrocities were rampant, including tit-for-tat mass killings in a fractious conflict fueled by a scramble for oil and the global politics of the Cold War.[45]

Sudan's official press agency reported, for instance, that SPLA forces had "massacred 83 people" including hospital patients in Yirol in 1986.[46] In 1987, militias armed by the Sudanese government massacred "Dinka tribesmen" in the town of Wau. Hundreds, maybe thousands, more civilians were slain by Sudanese security forces at Daein.[47] In 1989 and 1990, more than 2,000 southern Sudanese were killed by government militia at Jebelien. SPLA forces, some reportedly led by Salva Kiir, attacked villages of the Murle tribe in 1988 and 1989 and the area around Magwi in 1992 where they engaged in "looting, raping, and killing."[48] In 1991, after Riek Machar had split from Garang's SPLA and was fighting against it, Nuer forces loyal to him and armed Nuer youth known as the "White Army" attacked Dinka communities in and around Garang's hometown of Bor, slaughtering thousands of civilians.[49] Two years later, Rory Nugent of the *Observer* reported that Machar's forces were left to bury hundreds of civilians in the villages of Ayod, Yuai, Pathai, and Parvai who had been massacred by SPLA troops.[50] And so it went.

A PhD from Bradford Polytechnic in Great Britain and the most highly educated Nuer among the rebels, Machar later reconciled with the SPLA and was with them when a peace deal ended the civil war in 2005.[51] Under terms of the agreement, hashed out before Garang died in a helicopter crash, the people of southern Sudan voted for their independence in January 2011. Six months later, on July 9, South Sudan became the world's newest nation with President Kiir and Vice President Machar serving atop the government.[52]

The South Sudanese suffered, bled, and died for their independence, but they didn't win it alone. As John Kerry, then-chair of the Senate Foreign Relations Committee, put it in 2012, the United States "helped midwife the birth" of South Sudan.[53] From the mid-1980s onward, a bipartisan coalition in Washington and beyond championed the rebels and, in 1996, the U.S. began funneling military equipment to them through nearby Ethiopia, Eritrea, and Uganda.[54] As the new nation broke away from Sudan, the U.S. poured in billions of dollars in aid, including hundreds of millions of dollars of military and security assistance. It also sent military instructors to train the country's armed forces and advisors to mentor government officials.[55] On South Sudan's independence day, President Barack Obama hailed the moment as a "time of hope" and pledged U.S. partnership to the new land, emphasizing security and development.[56]

"For nearly a decade leading up to the 2011 declaration of independence, the cause of the nation and its citizens was one that was near and dear to the heart of two successive U.S. administrations and some of its most seasoned and effective thinkers and policymakers," Patricia Taft, a senior associate with the Fund for Peace, wrote in a 2014 analysis of South Sudan. "In order to secure this nation-building 'win,' both the George W. Bush and Obama administrations poured tons of aid into South Sudan, in every form imaginable. From military aid to food aid to the provision of technical expertise, America was South Sudan's biggest ally and backer, ardently midwifing the country into nationhood by whatever means necessary."[57]

For all America's efforts, the wheels started coming off almost immediately. "We've gotten pretty good at understanding what goes into building a state, institutionally, but as far as what creates a nation that's actually functional, we fell short," Taft tells me. The U.S., she says, failed to do the necessary heavy lifting to encourage the building of a shared national identity and sat on its hands when targeted interventions might have helped reverse worrisome developments.

"From the start, the cleavages between the leadership, represented by President Salva Kiir and former Vice President, Riek Machar, current leader of the opposition, were evident," Taft notes. "Decades of personal history, fraught with ugly political and tribal undercurrents, may have been temporarily shelved in the name of national unity but remained unresolved and simmering below the surface."[58]

In the years leading up to the war, Machar did express regret for the Bor massacre and apologized to those who lost family members. "Giving an apology is the best way of bringing in peace. We don't want to pass these painful things to our children," said the vice president, later adding: "So those of us who have survived and who [had] seen painful things during the war, we need to kick off the process of national reconciliation."[59] But no genuine reconciliation process ever began. As a result, South Sudan remained an infant state of submerged rage and deep suspicion filled with desperately poor people, lacking infrastructure, possessing only a sea of oil and too many men skilled in little beyond guerilla warfare. In other words, it was a powder keg with *when*, not *if*, stamped on it.

In 2013, Machar announced his intention to run against Kiir in the upcoming presidential elections. In response, Kiir sacked Machar as well as a group of former John Garang loyalists in high government posts. Tensions escalated through the fall. In December, Machar moved to challenge Kiir through the apparatus of the Sudan People's Liberation Movement, or SPLM, the political party to which they both belonged. When Kiir thwarted these efforts, Machar and the Garang faction walked out. Soon after, fighting began. Kiir called it a coup, while his opponents claimed it was a response to his efforts to disarm the Nuers in the Presidential Guard just across the street from Simon Wuor's home. The war has been raging ever since.

Looking back, UNMISS's Ibrahim Wani summed up the situation this way: "South Sudan had huge challenges. It was never a place where there was a strong sense of the rule of law. No respect for life. No basic rights. Depending on how you count, 20 or 50 years of civil war...Then they set up a government which had no tradition to build on. If anything, there were a lot of negative traditions, either from the way they conducted the war or what they inherited from Sudan. There were no institutions in place, a lot of very negative tendencies and you have a force that comes into power without any of the institutional restraints that safeguard human rights. And then there's a cultural tradition that is inimical to a lot of basic human rights...In the case of South Sudan, history suggests there is a problem with a cycle of impunity that needs to be broken. A lot of people refer to 1991 and say there were violations and nothing happened to the perpetrators. There was no investigation, no attempt at closure. And so it's not surprising that we see a repeat of the violence."

◆

In fact, it took only a few days for the Juba crisis of 2013 to wend its way northward, 200 kilometers, to the epicenter of 1991's horror: Bor. Around December 17, the forces of the local SPLA commander, General Peter Gadet—now on a U.S. sanctions list—defected to Machar's rebels, taking the majority of his troops, mostly Nuer, with him.[60] It wasn't long before gunfire again began to echo in the town.

Many said the attacks on Nuers in Juba were reprisals for the 1991 massacre and now, it seemed, Nuers were back in Bor eager to settle a days-old score and pay Dinkas back for Gudele and Jebel and Mia Saba, even though the residents of Bor had nothing to do with those killings, knew nothing about them, and were still grappling with their own losses, now two decades old.

Martha was one of them. When I meet her, she's wearing her

Sunday best: a red and black blouse, a long black skirt, and purple sandals with silver buckles. She has gold hoops in her ears and a large gold cross dangles from a chain around her neck. Her face is broad with lots of character. There's a quiet intensity about her. Martha suffered mightily during the civil war of the 1980s and 1990s. Her husband, like so many Dinkas in and around Bor, died in 1991 during what came to be known as the *ruon capoth* ("season of the lone survivor") when the town was almost emptied of inhabitants.[61]

Martha eventually fled to northern Sudan, only returning after independence. Life wasn't perfect or even easy, but overall things were good. Her 25-year-old daughter Ayak, a wisp of a young woman with a toothy smile and big brown eyes, lived with her and so did her grandchildren, a six-year-old girl and a boy of one and a half. After Juba exploded, another daughter, Nyanachiek, the mother of the two youngsters, called as she did every day. Usually, she just asked about the children and everyone's health, but not that day. She was in the capital and could see the writing on the wall. She told her mother to leave Bor immediately. To Martha, that was inconceivable, even when Nyanachiek broke down in tears, even when Ayak seconded her sister and suggested that they leave, when even the children already sensed something was terribly wrong. But Martha was adamant.

A government vehicle with a loudspeaker on top rolled through the streets telling people that the fighting in Juba wouldn't affect them. A neighbor, a Nuer, one of whose wives was a Dinka woman, told her not to worry. So Martha didn't worry and Martha didn't run.[62]

But many Dinkas did. They fled to the UNMISS base in Bor—500 of them on the 17th alone. The next day, Bor fell to the rebels and that afternoon, 12,500 civilians flooded into the U.N. encampment in just three hours.

Not Martha, though. She saw men in uniforms firing their weapons at each other. It was chaotic, but it was soldier-on-soldier violence. Her neighbor urged her to stay inside and they did. Huddled under the bed, Ayak told her niece and nephew that the gunshots were firecrackers, but there was no fooling them. So she played music for them on her phone, just to keep them calm.

Friends insisted that Martha take the children to the UNMISS base and not waste a second more. Nyanachiek called again, sobbing, pleading for them to leave. She had, she told them, stopped eating and was sick with worry. Still Martha refused. It would be over soon, she insisted. There was no need to run. Ayak was desperate, but would never leave her mother. "I lost my father in 1991. There was no way I would abandon my mother to die. I'd rather die with her," she tells me.[63]

By now, the Nuer rebels were running roughshod over the town, looting and pillaging, busting into banks to steal whatever cash was on hand, cleaning out shops, burning businesses and homes. "Do you want your life or the money," was the choice they offered a foreign shopkeeper.[64] Many weren't so lucky. Villages south of Bor were attacked and civilians executed. In one of them, Goy, at least four elderly people were shot dead and on the road there, everything was looted and burned by what was now being called Machar's "SPLA in Opposition."[65]

In Bor itself, things were only getting worse. Not only Dinka but other targeted ethnicities—Anyuak, Murle, Shilluk—and foreigners from Ethiopia, Eritrea, Kenya, and Uganda were fleeing any way they could, leaving only the elderly, the sick, the crippled, the mentally handicapped, and stragglers like Martha's family behind. Many of the aged and infirm stayed in the belief that they would slow down fleeing relatives and that, by virtue of their frailties, they would be spared by the rebels. The first assumption might have been true, the second was decidedly not. "On December 22nd," said a 40-year-old disabled war veteran who was living in Bor, "they killed two of my disabled colleagues, Piel Mayen, 65, and Keny Dabai, 40, both also veterans, as well as a mad person. They were in their homes when they were killed." Similarly, an old man in another neighborhood reported the killing of six of his elderly friends by Nuers.[66]

Though the violence was escalating, Martha still would not move. Finally, a relative who had fled to the UNMISS camp called to say that she had no choice. Nuer fighters were identifying Dinka civilians by their language and executing them. It didn't matter who you were or what condition you were in. Sitting tight meant certain death. Phone calls bounced from Bor to Juba and back again. Through a relative at the UNMISS camp, Nyanachiek got in touch with a young male cousin in Bor who, with his mother and other family members, had also been trying to ride out the violence. Thanks to a solar charger, he had a phone with plenty of juice, but no air time and no way to add minutes to his phone by buying one of the normally ubiquitous scratch cards, for 5, 10, or 25 South Sudanese pounds. From Juba, however, Nyanachiek bought and sent air time to her cousin and then coordinated a family exodus. He and his side of the clan would meet Martha, Ayak, and the two children at Saint Andrew's Episcopal Church. Whichever group arrived first would hide nearby and keep an eye out for the others. Once they all made it—if they all made it—they would make a dash for safety. The river seemed to be the only option.

Martha's brood got to the church first and stayed out of sight. The children were instructed to remain silent. "If you make noise, the soldiers will come here and shoot," Ayak told them. Rebels passed by. So did civilians who had already fled into the bush with nothing but the clothes on their backs. Now, some were sneaking back into town to look for food. The ones spotted by Nuers driving around in confiscated government Toyota SUVs were cut down by withering gunfire.

Finally, their cousin arrived and the united family, 18 in all, decided to make a run for it. They weren't the only ones. The last of Bor's able-bodied residents were also heading for the Nile as fast as they could. Next came a blur of violence spiked with chaos as Martha's and Ayak's memories seemed to shatter like glass: along the road, a house was burning, there were bodies, civilians, mostly men, but women and children, too. They pressed on, the Nuer rebels behind them and firing. "I saw someone being shot. First his head was there and then it wasn't," Martha remembered. As they got closer to the river, they passed a woman shot through the throat, still alive but clearly dying. Her baby sat next to her, wailing, but there was no stopping now. "We were running, so were many others. We couldn't stop. Many didn't make it. They died there," says Ayak.

Three large ferries sat near the shore of the Nile, boats so big they usually transport cattle as well as people across the river to Awerial County in Lakes State. This day, there were no cows and people were crowding aboard—people, that is, who had secured places in advance. Even now. Even with Nuer troops running them down, murdering them, unless you had a male relative who had secured a spot ahead of time, you were out of luck. A man they knew had bought passage for his relatives. He promised he'd get some of Martha's family on board, but all 18 of them was out of the question. By now, people were falling dead around them. Others were plunging into the water. Who lives and who dies? Who gets to cross the river and who faces death on shore? In the midst of the pandemonium came a decision. The elders and children were most vulnerable. Martha would take all eight children aboard and sail to the safety of Lakes State. The rest would stay and try to survive.

It seemed like a sensible plan, but it began to disintegrate almost as soon as it was made. The ferry drifted into deeper water as the rebels got closer and the gunfire intensified. Martha, who has no idea how old she is but looks to be in her 60s, doesn't move like she used to. So Ayak, slight and slender but far more agile, grabbed Nyanachiek's children and the daughter of her cousin and waded toward the ferry, struggling to keep the kids above water. She planned to deposit them on the boat, while her mother waded out on her own.

Gripped by fear, Martha's sister pulled the other five children back. And it soon became apparent that Martha wasn't going to make it onto the boat either. "You go instead," she called out to Ayak. "I'll try to run."

With her tiny nephew astride her shoulders, the water inching up to her neck, Ayak boosted the youngster aboard with help from those in the boat. The vessel was packed with people. The tiny boy was passed from hand to hand into the interior of the ferry, his cries drowned out by gunfire, the sound of the engine, and the din made by panicked people. The other two children were next. By the time Ayak clambered aboard, they were nowhere to be seen. But Nyanachiek's daughter had picked her way through the packed-in passengers, somehow finding her little brother and wrapping her arms around him. It took another 30 minutes for Ayak to gather all three kids amid a mass of crying, terrified passengers whose weight left the boat bogged down in the silt and grass of this marshy part of the Nile, forcing men to repeatedly leap into the cloudy brown water to help push it free.

As the rebels kept firing at the slow-moving targets, Ayak pulled the children down, taking cover as best she could. The other boats came under heavier sustained gunfire, she says, and people began to jump into the water. Who knows how many died leaping from the ferries or among the women and children—many of whom didn't know how to swim—who waded into the river in an attempt to avoid the bullets and never made it out, some pulled under by the Nile's current and swept away? A quick and dirty body count by local authorities indicated that around 300 people might have died this way.[67] From what she witnessed, Ayak believes it was many more. She saw only one survivor from the other vessels—a boy grasping the hand of a man aboard her boat and pulled along in the water as they moved further out into the river. A crossing that usually takes less than an hour took them four to five, she says, but her boat finally made it.

Left on the river bank, Martha and the others abandoned everything they had brought, even the solar phone charger, and began slogging through the marsh at river's edge, searching for a place to hide. They joined countless frantic families fleeing into shoreline swamps or to small islands in the river, and concealing themselves in the rushes and tall grass. Exhausted, sometimes submerged up to their noses, relentlessly bitten by insects wherever their skin was exposed, Martha's family struggled to keep silent as the rebels hunted down those in hiding.

The ordeal began at 8 a.m. By 3 p.m., the sounds of gunfire finally receded and the survivors started stirring, Martha and her kin among them. They now headed for the edge of town, running as fast as they could. Martha had no shoes. Her feet were already raw and bloody. When they could run no more, they walked on, in pain, with no food, for two days. Finally, a man drove up in a car. A friend of Nyanachiek's young male cousin was traveling with them and still had some money, so they were able to pay the man to drive them the rest of the way to the town of Pangol. Eventually, Martha found a spot aboard a plane headed for Juba.

As it turned out, Ayak's nightmare wasn't over once she crossed the Nile to Awerial County. There she was, a young woman with no money, no food, no shelter, no phone, and three traumatized children. Still, they were lucky in one respect. They found a spot under a tree. With masses of displaced people in the area—84,000 by early January—finding a prime piece of real estate was no small feat.[68] But her luck ended there. She was still stranded among marooned, desperate people in charge of two young girls and a toddler. For three days she struggled to stay awake, fearful that if she fell into a deep sleep, someone might take one of the children. Not that sleep would have come easily. As ferries continued to arrive from the other shore, Ayak waited, hoping to see her mother step off one of them, safe and unharmed. Each was another heartbreak. People claimed that those who hadn't crossed had all been executed. (Martha would hear a version of the same grim rumor: those in the boats had all been shot or had drowned.)

"I thought I'd never see my mother or my cousins again," Ayak tells me. Her mother echoes the feeling: "I thought I would never again see my daughter and my grandchildren."

Martha's group borrowed a phone and called a relative to let the family know they were alive. Ayak also borrowed a phone and got in touch with a cousin who passed along the good news: Martha had survived and was on the move. Ayak thought they were just telling her what she wanted—needed—to hear to keep her sane and the children safe. Finally, Nyanachiek got a fix on her younger sister's location and found a man driving north from Juba. She bought herself a place in his car and on the third day, Ayak and she were reunited. A day later, both of them squeezed into the same car, now making the return trip, arriving there on

December 27, the same day a plane carrying Martha landed in the capital.[69]

◆

Meanwhile, the situation in Bor took another set of turns. On Christmas Day, SPLA troops drove Machar and Gadet's forces from the town; then, on December 31, with support from untrained but well-armed Nuer White Army youths, the rebels retook the town. It would change hands yet again on January 18, when Ugandan soldiers, sent to reinforce Kiir's troops, pushed the rebels out.

Something dark, even for this war, awaited the first returnees. "There were bodies all over town—in the hospital, in the market, in the streets," says UNMISS's Ibrahim Wani, who was there. "When you drove through at that time, you couldn't miss the bodies." Skye Wheeler, the author of Human Rights Watch's seminal reports on atrocities during the conflict, was shocked. "Bor was the worst. I've never been anywhere that bad in my entire life," she tells me. "There were dead bodies everywhere. The whole town was a massive crime scene."[70]

"Crime scene," is an apt description for what was discovered at Saint Andrew's Episcopal Church, where Martha and her family gathered for their escape from town. By Christmas Day, around 15 to 20 elderly men and women had taken refuge in the church compound, hoping to find sanctuary. Armed young men arrived sometime between the rebel takeover on December 31 and the first weeks of January. They lined up the elderly and shot most of them, according to a survivor. Fourteen bodies were reportedly found on the church grounds. When Skye Wheeler arrived on the scene in late January, she still saw 11 corpses scattered about.

I arrive at Saint Andrew's a little more than a year later and, of course, there's no obvious sign of the carnage that took place here. The church—a squat, hangar-length crème-colored building with blue metal doors—is locked, but its choir, a group of women and girls in colorful skirts and headwraps, are lined up singing and dancing in unison near the back of a compound under the shade of a leafy tree. They're arrayed according to height, six rows of six women each, little girls up front, women more than 6 feet tall in the back. A very tall man in a blue and white striped dress shirt and gray pants stands to the side, appraising them. Another man, in a long-sleeve blue shirt and tan pants, is standing at a keyboard next to the trunk of the tree, accompanying them. Not far away is a fenced-in area with a sign announcing a December 2014 event honoring "fallen fellow citizens and victims 1991–2014." It urges participants to rise "above your tribal boundaries for peace."

I've visited a lot of monuments to mass killings—in Asia, Europe, and the United States. They can take many different forms: a room filled with human hair, an ossuary of skulls, or simply a statue on a pedestal. Here, there are two individual tombs, the size and shape of coffins, topped with metal crosses. One seems covered mainly by ordinary beige flooring tiles. The other is overlaid with smaller white and green bathroom tiles. Behind these sits a much larger monument positioned over a mass grave. Atop a black concrete base about a foot high is a 12-foot by 24-foot white slab overlaid with a tiled cross of muted beige, orange, and tan. On top of that is a large angled plinth, the type that might support a memorial plaque, though presently there is none. I stare at the unmarked monuments, listen to the singing of the parishioners, think about the last moments of the dead collected here. "They're not supposed to kill old ladies," a woman who said she survived the attack told reporter Jessica Hatcher.[71]

They're not supposed to kill the sick and injured either. But in the nearby Bor State Hospital, the attackers executed a woman in her bed. Other bodies were scattered about the grounds. An assessment team from Médecins Sans Frontières (MSF) was told that 14 patients were shot and killed in the hospital, along with a driver working for the Ministry of Health. The MSF team saw the decomposed corpses of a woman and child in a water tank on the hospital grounds.[72] Journalists who visited the compound on January 19 counted eight bodies inside the hospital, including a woman shot in her bed.[73]

I travel to a perhaps even darker site down the road from the church and hospital. We pull over at a nondescript spot and two local officials lead the way. "You're not afraid to go in here are you?" one of them asks.

The sun is bright and baking as I begin threading my way through piles of loose dirt, trying to avoid stepping on tightly packed, rudimentary graves. A cross of two twigs feebly lashed together has clearly fallen from the top of one of the mounds; at the foot of another lie purple artificial flowers. More elaborate concrete tombs with hand-painted markers, one of them adorned with decorative tiles, another white-washed, stand off to my left. I advance through a tangled field of weeds, now brittle and golden in the heat, past crushed beer cans and plastic bottles, some half charred or melted.

They call this out-of-the way field Langbar, after a type of tree that grows here. There's evidence that a fire ran wild at some point, leaving singed stalks and stumps behind. Briefly, I find myself in a small stretch that the flames didn't touch, then the blackened landscape begins again. In one unburnt area, there are raised mounds of dirt overgrown by thickets of prickly scrub and grasses dried to a crisp in the unrelenting heat. Ahead of me, something gleams in the sun, a bright white orb amid the ebony expanse.

There are four mass graves here, four collections of Bor's dead—men, women, and children whose bodies were found in the streets or in homes; men, women, and children running or hiding, pleading or cowering when the armed men came upon them. I'm told that one of these graves contains 179 corpses—75 men, 70 women, 27 children, and 7 corpses so badly decomposed or burned or mutilated that it was impossible to discern age or sex. Another holds 162 people—62 men, 56 women, 32 children, 12 unknowns. The third is the resting place for 135 bodies—61 men, 41 women, 17 children, 16 unknowns. The final one holds 46 bodies—23 men, 17 women, and 6 children.

I've been shown photos of the 2014 burial here: a huge trench dug by a bulldozer; bodies shrouded in white, lined up, and placed in an immense pit, head-to-toe, three corpses across. It's impossible to tell precisely where one grave ends and the next begins. There are no markers. In a few years, it may be impossible to identify graves at all.

The orb in the sun-scalded field turns out to be a human skull, or rather half of one, sitting upright, tilted to the left. Its remaining empty eye socket stares up at me. The men who guided me here point to it and other bones littering an area not far away as evidence of the scale of the killing, of the unfortunate fates of those who had no families left here to bury them. I simply nod. It's impossible, of course, to know the provenance of a lone partial skull in a rudimentary burial ground like this one. But it certainly evokes the sense of horror that this town just can't seem to shake. Bor might be the Guernica of South Sudan if, that is, German pilots had slaughtered five to ten times the number of Spaniards killed in that town in 1937 and came back to do it again 22 years later.[74]

And keep in mind that the bodies in these mass graves represent only a fraction of the deaths in this town during its most recent crisis. Local authorities state that 2,007 people were killed in Bor County. The U.N. found that to be a "reasonable estimate."[75] The dead reside, the town's mayor tells me, in 1,140 individual or mass graves. He says another 307 drowned in the river. Then there are 25 people still considered missing. They could have been kidnapped, he confides, or they may simply have been killed. No one knows.

For the second time in a quarter-century, Bor had borne the brunt of the very worst of war. Satellite images showed almost 2,000 residential properties and nearly 100 commercial structures were destroyed, including the town market.[76] The amount of damage and the scale of the suffering were immense, undeniable, irrefutable. Still, I want to know more.

I locate one of the Nuer rebels in the force that took and lost, retook and re-lost Bor, though to hear this young officer tell it, the defeats were merely "strategic withdrawals." He does give his full name, but asks that, under the circumstances, I use only his first name: Ruot.

Ruot wears a checkered shirt with a black t-shirt underneath, brown pants, and bright green flip-flops. His head is shaved, his demeanor serious, and he's all about contradictions. Tall and athletic looking, he walks with a cane and a limp, thanks to the bullet that transformed him from soldier to veteran. He looks about 18, but swears he's 28. He wants peace, justice, and accountability but, like so many Nuers, he also wants Machar to be president.

An SPLA soldier at the time of the Juba crisis, Ruot says that, initially, he hoped it was just a battle between isolated groups of soldiers or a strictly political battle and he tells me of the "pain in his heart" when he heard that his people were being killed in the capital. By his own account, he had little trouble turning from an SPLA soldier into a rebel in the course of a day. His explanation is eloquent: "When I first heard of the killings of Nuer women, children, and men, I felt angry and upset, as a man, as a soldier. I was being paid by the government and the government was killing my people. I decided it's better to go rescue my people than serve the government and take their money. People are created by God, not by the government. We, Nuer people, are the second largest community in South Sudan. If the president says he wants to remove us from the earth, then we will fight. It's better to fight and die than to simply accept it. It's better to fight than to serve this government and take their money. People are more important than money."

Ruot then regales me with his account of the various battles for Bor, of rebel triumphs and—he goes out of his way to emphasize—of the exemplary behavior of his side toward civilians. I press him about attacks on Dinka noncombatants. He insists that his rebels not only protected Dinkas, but also escorted them to the UNMISS camp, treating them well along the way. There is, indeed, evidence that such acts did occur amid the mass killings, the burnings, the destruction. What about all the bodies?

Since he and his rebel comrades were obviously upset by the violence in Juba, didn't they want to teach the Dinkas a lesson? But he won't be goaded. No matter how I put it, the answer is the same. He blames the destruction on the SPLA forces when they retook the town. I cite the testimony of Dinka residents like Martha and Ayak. He won't budge.

This is the dilemma, the bone in the throat, the point that can't be gotten past. All sides profess to want true justice—as long as it means their side comes out on top. I've written Ruot off as hopelessly partisan until I ask what needs to be done to achieve justice and accountability. Facing such a question, people on all sides to the conflict repeatedly mention calling on the Hague-based International Criminal Court (ICC)—but only in terms of prosecuting the opposing tribal leader. Many Dinkas want Machar in the dock; many Nuers want to see Kiir there. Ruot wants to send them both. Intrigued, I ask him to explain. It seems that he envisions the court as an arbiter that will, in a Solomon-like fashion, send one man to prison or the gallows and the other home to rule. In his mind, there's no question which man will prevail. Still, sending both men to the court? Perhaps it would be a starting point.[77]

Martha, whose town has twice been ravaged by the forces of Riek Machar, sees it differently. "Take him to the world court," she says. "He's a criminal. He needs to go there. I don't know why they let Riek, why they let the Nuers, kill people every time?"

Her daughter Nyanachiek agrees. During one of our chats, she wears a dark green dress with delicate cap sleeves. Her hair is pulled back revealing gold crescents adorning her ears. She's quick to smirk, but a smile needs to be earned. Her voice is like molasses; her English measured and deliberate. She never went to school for it, but learned it by listening in her uncle's home. She tells me exactly how she feels about the former vice president.

"To be a leader, you have to be respected by your people. But that respect is gone and I don't think he can get it back." She notes that there are now people who lost their parents to Machar's forces in 1991 and their children to his troops in 2013. "If Riek Machar is given what he wants and is made president, what about those who lost their families—what will they think?" she asks. "He may say this or that but all I know is that he's a killer."

She adds that she simply can't understand why African leaders and world powers support Machar. (No matter which side a person you interview is on, he or she is almost guaranteed to claim that the country's African neighbors and the West support the other side.) "Any other Nuer is okay. Any leader can be the president, but not Riek." Maybe his son, she later says, but never him.

Her younger sister Ayak picks up on the point. "If he had waited for the election and had not started this crisis, then maybe we would have elected him. But after what he did now? Never, ever." She recalls Riek's contrition in the years before the 2013 crisis. "When Riek became vice president, he wrote a letter to the people of Bor to apologize for what happened in 1991. He asked for forgiveness. And yet, he did the very same thing, again. And if a new peace agreement is signed, he'll send another message and say 'I'm sorry' again. I'm not saying that they [Nuers] are bad people, but I think there's something wrong with their minds… All the time, they are fighting, fighting, fighting."[78]

More than a year after fleeing Bor, Nyanachiek's young daughter gets angry if you so much as mention its name. When Ayak questions her niece about returning to the town, the little girl insists that she'll never go back. Nyanachiek asked her why and, she says, her daughter told her: "There's too much shooting, too much running, too much hiding. I don't ever want to go back to Bor."

The road to Bor is littered with lifeless vehicles, abandoned to the bush, rusting wrecks that tell a tale of poor infrastructure, scant government services, and the fragility of technology in the face of a hostile environment. Here you find a burnt-out minivan. There lies a rusting remnant of a box truck or the skeletal chassis of a broken-down tanker truck, or what remains of an old flatbed. Past the midway point from Juba, I see an overturned sedan and wonder how it made it this far on a dirt track so rutted that's it's fit only for trucks and 4x4 SUVs like the Toyota Land Cruiser I'm riding in.

Then there are the tanks, rusting metal hulks of uncertain vintage and provenance, stranded in a gully by a bridge or sitting off the side of the roadway. Some of these big-gunned behemoths look as if they might have seen action in the civil war that began in the 1950s or the war that raged through the 1980s, 1990s, and 2000s. These aren't, mind you, blasted wrecks laid low by air power or rocket-propelled grenades. They're intact vehicles that seemingly just stopped running at some point. And how, in South Sudan, do you tow a tank? The simple answer is: you don't. You leave it there, a monument to a military struggle that never seems to be over, an eternal reminder of the deadly campaigns that have shaped this country over the last century.

By the time we're three-quarters of the way to Bor, I'm no longer shocked when one of these orphaned metal monsters comes into view—until, that is, I spy a unique one off to the right. Unlike the drab, weathered tanks we've passed by, this one is painted in a camouflage pattern so bright and unsuited to the surrounding vegetation that there's no chance of its blending in. It appears to be of such recent vintage that I'd hardly be shocked if its drive sprockets, road wheels, and tracks suddenly sprang to life and the many-tonned monster promptly lumbered off into the bush. It reminds me that I'm on a road that was a war zone a little more than a year ago. After opposition forces took Bor, they pushed south toward the capital, only to be met by SPLA and Ugandan troops and the Ugandan Air Force.[79] The rebel advance was halted. Later, U.N. personnel found evidence that those planes had dropped banned cluster munitions, an indiscriminate weapon that regularly claims the lives of civilians in post-conflict zones across the world. Both South Sudan and Uganda denied their use, but in this war denials are a dime a dozen.[80] I get out of the Land Cruiser to take a look at the tank but, remembering these claims and denials, decide not to chance leaving the road.

The fighting on this route may be past, but soldiers remain. All along the way, in *bomas* (villages) and *payams* (collections of villages), we stop at military and police checkpoints—usually little more than lengths of string or rope, sometimes with a few makeshift flags attached, stretched across the road. At some posts, we find all the troops bedded down on mats, fast asleep in these early morning hours. Sometimes, a groggy soldier rises, stretches, scratches, staggers to the roadside, loosens the rope from a tree limb and lets us through. Sometimes, the men request "water." They don't, of course, *mean* water, but they prefer not to say what they really want. Still, it's plenty clear and 10 South Sudanese pounds—enough to buy ten bottles of water in Juba—does the trick. At one checkpoint, the man with the Kalashnikov inquiring about water is a lot less scary than the one behind him with a large curved knife yelling, "Water! Water!" I'm hoping he's drunk. If not, he's deranged. My driver can't get the money out fast enough for me. As we pull away, the man with the gun and the man with the knife are squabbling over the "water" we've provided.

Most of the endlessly jarring ride to (and from) Bor is otherwise uneventful. Speed bumps protecting sections of this meandering earthen road force us to slow down as we pass through villages, allowing a glimpse of them as they spring to morning life. Women with short-handled brooms assiduously sweep the dirt in front of their *tukuls*. Small cooking fires flicker to life. In some areas we brake or swerve as gaunt goats trot across the roadway or we thread our way around confused, scrawny, dirty-beige sheep and through groups of large, white, lyre-horned cattle and smaller cows with less flamboyant appendages.

Rain in the mid-morning turns sections of the road a rich, deep crimson and helps quell the clouds of dust kicked up by big trucks hauling water or food or, in one case, huge U.N. armored vehicles. But soon enough the sun emerges and an SPLA pickup truck with two young soldiers standing in its bed, rifles slung on their backs, rockets past in the opposite direction, leaving a trail of dust that we seem to be eating for the next five minutes. Soon after, a civilian pickup with a huge, jagged hole in the center of the now ill-named windshield, does the same. Sometimes we're driving almost completely blind, and yet we, too, jolt along at a remarkably fast clip, careening from one side of the road to the other, trying to follow the flattest path possible, bumping and bouncing through a scrubby landscape stretching to the horizon.

It's late morning when we arrive in Bor, a mostly one-story town whose sprawling market hugs both sides of the main drag and boasts food, phones, and lodgings. There's the Modern Hotel that doesn't exactly live up to its name, the swank-looking Safari Hotel, with its fresh, bright green paint job, that appears ready to snap up any American dollars or South Sudanese pounds proferred by NGO donor groups passing through. Then there's the ramshackle-looking Obama Inn, happily trading on the American president's name. We pass them all, as well as the intriguingly named Big Man Restaurant, but keep on driving to a low-slung, beige office building, the seat of the town's municipal government.

Traditional African "big men" demonstrate their status by belly girth and the feeding of their followers.[81] I soon find myself with the town's preeminent big man, an official who lives up to the title. Plenty tall and impressively wider than the coterie of men who surround him, he talks to me for a time in his office, then instructs me to follow his two-car caravan packed with his clique and one young, camouflage-clad bodyguard.

Soon we arrive at tall, purple metal gates. Carrying a swagger stick, the big man emerges from his Toyota Land Cruiser and ushers me inside. We sit down at a table beside a sprawling peach-colored house under the welcome shade of the only large tree in sight. I'm seated between the big man, who is togged out in a flashy blue suit, a red power tie, and a leather cowboy hat, and a two-star general in desert camouflage fatigues. Nearby, two men from his entourage clad in business attire—pink and purple dress shirts, respectively—wrestle, each trying to grab the other's leg and upend him. An animated crowd of onlookers laugh and whoop and cheer. Four eight-foot-tall ostriches reluctantly make way for the grapplers.

The business card of the big man with the swagger stick reads "Hon. Eng. Nhial Majak Nhial." He's the mayor of Bor. This is his house and those around the table are his entourage and these are his ostriches. "They're only chicks," he assures me.

Nhial's dress and accoutrements evoke the style of President Salva Kiir. His face is round. His cheeks still resemble those of a chubby child. His neck is thick. A scruff of beard clings to his chin, petering out along his jawline only to reestablish itself near his sideburns. He sports a slight paunch, but his build is powerful. He's seen a lot for a young mayor. Twice his town has fallen to rebel forces and twice he had to flee for his life. He tells me of the looting of his father's home and adds that he's alive thanks to luck and the quick actions of the SPLA. While he now projects self-assurance, he proceeds to fill me in on the crisis of confidence he experienced upon returning to what was left of his town in January 2014, the day after the SPLA won it back.

After surveying the damage, he headed to Juba and was named acting governor of Jonglei State (in which Bor is located), but suddenly found himself paralyzed by fear. "Especially after seeing the massacres in the church and the hospital—I saw a great deal of inhumanity—after what was done to the civilians. The whole town was unlivable and it looked like it would be for a long time," he confides. "So I had a very difficult time. I spent two days locked in a hotel room. I didn't go out once. I didn't know what to do. That's when the idea of resigning first came into my mind."

His story soon takes a hairpin turn for the triumphant, however, with his return home to Bor. "Yes, I even thought of resigning from my position to find another way to help the people. But when I shared these thoughts with the people and the leadership of the town, they said there was no better way for me to help the people of Bor than to stay in office. The whole community was looking up to me to help them."

Nhial has come to believe, he tells me, that divine intervention may even have been at play. "I think that God gave me a mission to clean up Bor town. So, we cleaned up the dead bodies, bodies that had been decaying for over a month. We completed this cleaning of Bor town by the end of March, the beginning of April. It was the most difficult task of my lifetime, a task I never imagined I could do... I thank God because God gave me the strength and I thank the people of Bor. I don't even have the words to express my thanks because without their support, I wouldn't have managed to collect the bodies," he recalls. "By doing this, we planted the seeds of peace. We prevented anarchy and revenge and even genocide."

"We had to hide the past by collecting all the remains," he reflects, bringing up the specter of reprisals against the Nuer community for the devastation of Bor. "There would still be a lot of killing here today because if people see the bones of relatives that were inhumanely killed, then it will incite a feeling of revenge. So the peace and tranquility of Bor are owed to the people who collected the remains of their loved ones and fellow citizens and buried them with honor."[82]

Nhial boasts that most of the population has now returned and indeed Bor is once again a bustling urban center and still one of the largest towns in South Sudan. Even Ayak has returned. But Nyanachiek's children and her mother are hardly alone in staying away. Nhial tells me that Bor's 2013 population of perhaps 350,000 in 2013 has been reduced to about 200,000.

At his office, Nhial spoke soaringly of peace and even a willingness to see Machar return to the government to placate the international community. Now, at home, as lunch ends, he gets animated and begins to expound. Spurred by a question of mine, he sets off on a long monologue stoked only by my intermittent requests for clarification. He talks of conspiracies: of the U.N. aiding, directly or indirectly, Machar's forces; of the international community backing the rebel leader despite the blood on his hands. "As we speak today," he declares "rebel forces in uniform are being delivered food. Most of this aid that is being brought by UNMISS, that is being collected from the Western countries, that is being brought by the World Food Program is being used to feed the rebels and allow them to attack civilians."

And he doesn't leave out the United States, either. "Riek Machar is being supported by Washington... UNMISS and the Western world are supporting this person to come back to the government, but he's actually just like Boko Haram, ISIS, and al Shabab!" he exclaims. UNMISS never responds to my questions about Nhial's accusations. A report by the Small Arms Survey, a Geneva-based independent research group, issued a few months after I speak to Nhial shines a light on small arms and ammunition lost by or diverted from U.N. forces and other peacekeepers in South Sudan. Indeed, quantities of both have inadvertently been lost to armed groups.[83] UNMISS doesn't offer comment on that report, either.

By now, Nhial is essentially on stage, playing to his deputies, to the general, and to me specifically by dipping into what he knows of American history. He offers an analogy I never saw coming. "We have always accepted Riek Machar back to the leadership of South Sudan, but he's actually the Benedict Arnold of South Sudan." He raises an eyebrow, clearly expecting a flash of recognition on my face. Truth be told, the last time I heard mention of the revolutionary-general-cum-turncoat, the man who conspired to surrender the Continental Army's post at West Point to the British in 1780, was probably grammar school.

Nhial prods to see if I get the reference. "Yes, he's America's most famous traitor," I respond, leaving aside the fact that every man he betrayed in the colonies' rebel army was also a traitor to king and country. Nhial proceeds to construct a scenario that sounds like a treatment for a bad History Channel/SyFy mashup miniseries. "Today, in America, if Benedict Arnold was resurrected from his grave and said America would be better if he, Benedict Arnold, instead of Mr. Obama were the leader, I think Americans would go to the bush," Nhial explains.

I roll this scenario around in my brain and find myself picturing a zombie Benedict Arnold holding forth on FOX News. What, in the end, strikes me most is that Nhial knows enough about America to bring up Benedict Arnold, but not quite enough to realize that while Americans might head for the hills or some mountain redoubt, or go up-country, or into the wilderness, or off the grid, the one place no American will ever bug out to is "the bush." I simply nod, mutter something vague about apt analogies, and he continues to happily hold forth.

"Washington and the Western world are saying the Benedict Arnold of South Sudan should be made the president," he says, and proceeds to excoriate the U.S. for supposedly backing Machar. As he does, what comes to mind are the many interviews I've done with Nuers who are similarly indignant about supposed U.S. backing for Salva Kiir. Just two days before my trip to Bor, in fact, I sat down with 31-year-old Kueth Gatkuoth, another man itching to give me a piece of his mind. While he didn't reach back to colonial times, this Nuer man had plenty to say about the current U.S. leadership.

"I blame the government of America. The actions of the international community are in their hands. When the crisis in South Sudan erupted, the president, Salva Kiir, killed only members of our tribe—the men, the women, and the children, the innocent people... but then John Kerry arrived last year and recognized the legitimacy of the president and everything became worse."[84]

Indeed, in May 2014, and a number of times after, Secretary of State Kerry emphasized that Kiir was "constitutionally elected and duly elected by the people" and that there is no equivalency between his government and "a rebel force that is engaged in use of arms in order to seek political power or to provide a transition."[85] (A few months after Gatkuoth and I spoke, Kerry would appear on Eye Radio and condemn both Kiir and Machar. "What is happening is disgraceful," he said, noting that the Obama administration was "fed up with this avoidance of responsibility by the so-called leaders of this conflict on both sides" and that both men needed "to come to their senses.")[86]

At first, Gatkuoth was too angry at America to speak with me, but he finally decided that I offered him a chance to air his grievances. As his tirade picks up steam, there's no space for me to ask a question or seek further elaboration of anything. He insists that Kiir is practically a dictator and asks, purely rhetorically, if an American president would be considered a legitimate leader after slaughtering his own people. "The U.S. government is happy to enjoy democracy inside the United States, but they don't seem to care if the people of South Sudan are deprived of democracy. President Obama saw that President Kiir killed civilians on the basis of their tribe and then he invited President Kiir to enjoy dinner with him in the United States."[87]

This, too, is true. August 2014, decked out in his signature cowboy hat, Kiir was one of several dozen African leaders who attended a White House conference and lavish dinner, complete with a salad of produce from the first lady's garden, chilled spiced tomato soup, and grilled dry-aged Wagyu beef.[88] "This city, this house, has welcomed foreign envoys and leaders for more than two centuries. But never before have we hosted a dinner at the White House like this, with so many presidents, so many prime ministers all at once," President Obama said in his toast. "So we are grateful for all the leaders who are in attendance... Tonight we are making history, and it's an honor to have all of you here."[89] (In July 2015, Obama would finally take both Kiir and Machar to task for not showing "any interest in sparing their people from... suffering, or reaching a political solution.")[90]

By now, Gatkuoth is in a lather, repeating his points endlessly. I just nod, while he suddenly launches forth on the subject of the rebel leader who looms over all such conversations: "The reason why the whole Nuer community is rallying behind Dr. Riek Machar is not because we want him to become the president of South Sudan. It's because our relatives were killed just because they are Nuer. Dr. Riek says this is wrong and he's fighting... we want to join him so that we can avenge our loved ones who were killed. We're planning our revenge because the U.S. government and the international community say President Kiir is legitimate, even after killing his own people. What can we do? We must take revenge for our loved ones, our relatives." And so it went.

I snap myself out of the memory of Gatkuoth's angry interview and back to the current one in which Mayor Nhial continues to savage Machar. Near me, the mayor's minions are in a fight of their own, battling the nosy, hungry ostrich chicks to a draw. They repeatedly punch the birds in the neck or head when they try to steal food off a plate or simply get too close for comfort, but the ostriches are tough and bold. Even when they're given a swift kick or a lightning fast jab to the eye, they only back off momentarily. Soon enough, the enormous flightless fowl return to steal morsels of meat or beans or bits of whatever that green stew is.

Meanwhile, there's no stopping Nhial. Like Gatkuoth, he's riled and racing and now hanging on to his favorite analogy for dear life. "When we fought for the liberation of this country, this man—Riek Machar—turned his guns against the people of South Sudan... We won our independence and, for the sake of unity, we accepted the Benedict Arnold of South Sudan to become the vice president of this country." But Machar tried to take the presidency by force. "Just because it's not successful doesn't mean that it's not a coup d'état, but Washington and its allies have refused to accept this... Do not force him down the throats of the people of South Sudan. By encouraging the Benedict Arnold of South Sudan to become the president, you are encouraging anarchy." Nhial stops for a moment, suddenly turns to his inner circle and offers them a succinct explanation of just who Benedict Arnold is.

Then he's back to me. "The U.S. disowned Benedict Arnold forever until he died in London, yes?" I nod. "If the U.S. cannot accept your traitors, then how can we accept our traitors?" And then, just as suddenly, he pivots back into magnanimous statesman mode. "For the sake of the unity of the people of South Sudan, we will accept Mr. Riek Machar." But just quickly his voice becomes somber and low. "He should repent for the lives he has continuously cost us and his lack of shame over his betrayal of the people of South Sudan. He will go down in history as the most disgraced figure in our history... his name is smeared with the blood of the innocent people of South Sudan."

I ask Nhial if he thinks that Machar should stand trial. "He should have already been called to the ICC, but on behalf of the people, I don't say that he should be charged. Because if he's charged, if he's held accountable, the international community will say that we don't like peace." What, I ask, about the killings of Nuers that kicked off the violence in the capital? "If there were targeted killings in Juba, they should be investigated," he replies, "There should be no targeted killings of innocent Nuer civilians. Innocents from any tribe deserve nothing but protection."

But the question Nhial nor anyone else has answer to is this: Where can 115,000 people stuck on U.N. bases for more than a year and too afraid to go home find protection from the government forces that killed their relatives, friends, and neighbors and then looted, burned, or occupied their houses? What should they do, when government forces—so I'm repeatedly told—harass them if they leave their U.N. camps?[91]

Hoth Gor Luak is the chairman of one of these camps, Protection of Civilians (POC) Site #1 at U.N. House in Juba. A scarified Nuer elder with haunted, rheumy eyes and a snowy-white beard, he presides over what is now something close to an open-air prison. Behind razor wire and earthen berms, he lives alongside thousands of similarly marooned people. Theirs is a world of reeking latrines constructed of blue and white plastic sheeting and foul-smelling open sewers that flow past sweltering white plastic–tarp homes branded with the logo and initials of the International Organization for Migration. In tall guard towers looming above their sprawling settlement, bored, blue-helmeted U.N. troops stand eternal watch. Rudimentary stores, cobbled together with wood, plastic, and chicken wire, sell bottled water or snack crackers or vegetable oil or cell phone airtime. In a butcher shop, a quarter of a goat hangs amid a swarm of flies in the 100-degree heat.

People cluster in any shade that can be found. Men squat amid refuse in a bone-dry drainage ditch to take advantage of a rare tree that blocks the sun. Children lean against shipping containers just to linger briefly in their shadow. Water tanker trucks rumble by. A woman hovers over an enormous silver bowl of steaming rice, stirring it up with a huge silver spoon. A skinny man in a yellow tank top sits in the sun repairing a battered sandal. Women pass by balancing bright yellow jerry cans of water on their heads.

Many of the men in the camp wile away their days beneath open-faced plastic shelters. They stew. They argue. They go stir crazy. They get drunk or high. They start fights. When U.N. police rush to intervene, they are sometimes attacked with machetes and spears. One day I'm in the cavernous building known as Hangar #5 that sometimes serves as Luak's office (and on other occasions doubles as a church or a community center) when he gets a call on his cell phone. A fight has broken out somewhere in the camp. The chairman collects the relevant information and dispatches men to help calm the situation. I should, he advises me, stay in the hangar or better yet head back to the U.N. reception area to wait things out. I tell him I'm fine, though visiting journalists have been stoned in the camps and the U.N. has confiscated hundreds of weapons from iron bars to pistols to AK-47s.[92] Still, I convince Luak I'll be okay and head off to spend another day talking with the people stranded here.

One blazing afternoon a few weeks later, he and I sit in the shrinking shade just outside the hangar and chat for a while. Luak wants to give me some background on the conflict. The timbre of his voice betrays his age, but his speech is lively, animated, and conveys a special urgency. I lean back in my beige plastic chair and listen.

"The Dinkas have been in power from the 1950s until today. They don't want any other tribe to take power… The Dinkas believe that we want to kill them… But we, the Nuers, we know human rights. We have humanity. This was a fight and people fought and now it's over. We want to develop our country."

War has shaped most of Luak's life. He was involved in the long revolutionary struggle to free southern Sudan, only to witness his country consumed by still another war in his twilight years. But curiously enough, he remains an optimist, convinced that South Sudan still has a chance for a brighter future if, and only if, a grass-roots initiative replaces long, drawn-out peace talks taking place in Addis Ababa, Ethiopia. One ceasefire after another forged there between Kiir and Machar has gone down in flames—sometimes within hours of being signed. Luak has a better suggestion.

"Our country spent almost 50 years fighting. But we're lucky. We have oil, which we can use to develop our country. But in the mind of Dinkas, they always fear that, if peace comes, they will lose the power and maybe even their lives. This is their fear…," he says. Luak tells me that the politicos hashing out the crash-and-burn armistices in Addis Ababa have no incentive to bring the civil war to a quick close. "If these talks had been carried out by chiefs from the villages—the Nuer chiefs, the Dinka chiefs—if they would have been involved in these talks… we could have reached a better solution," he explains. "They would have come to a solution because the people who are dying are their children. Salva and his people don't have children here, their children are overseas… so they're not losing anything. The children who are dying are the children of other people. If they were losing their own children, they would have realized that this [war] is a mistake."[93]

◆

"I've never been a soldier," I say to the wide-eyed, lanky-limbed veteran sitting across from me. "Tell me about military life. What's it like?" Osman looks up as if the answer can be found in the blazing blue sky above, shoots me a sheepish grin, and then fixes his gaze on his feet. I let the silence wash over us and wait. He looks embarrassed. Perhaps it's for me.

Interviews sometimes devolve into these awkward, hushed moments. I've talked to hundreds of veterans over the years. Many have been reluctant to discuss their tours of duty for one reason or another. It's typical. But this wasn't the typical veteran— at least not for me.

Osman put in three years of military service, some of it during wartime. He saw battle and knows the dull drudgery of a soldier's life. He had left the army just a month before I met him.

Osman is 15 years old.

Children are central to the conflict in South Sudan. They suffer disproportionately—dying violently or succumbing to privation and endless preventable diseases their tiny bodies are ill-equipped to handle. But that's hardly all. About 13,000 children are also serving with the SPLA or the Sudan People's Liberation Army in Opposition, or with other militias and armed groups jockeying for power.[94]

Osman was lucky. He was one of more than 1,700 children demobilized by a rebel militia known as the Cobra faction that had been at war with the government.

I meet Osman in Pibor, an out-of-the-way town about 270 kilometers from Juba. The temperature here seems harsher, the air drier and dustier than in the capital. The days leave you feeling sapped and shriveled. The sun forces your eyes into a perpetual squint and the wind blows hot—unnaturally hot, blast-furnace hot.

The ground in Pibor is parched to the point of cracking. The gray moonscape has shattered into a spider's web of crevices, fissures, and clefts tailor-made for wrenching knees and toppling chairs when you shift your weight. Then there are the flies. Swarms of flies. Everywhere. I've experienced flies before, flies you can't keep off your food; so many that you cease swatting them and call a truce; so many that you agree to share your plate and your fork with them; so much sharing that they might become part of your meal if they fail to flit away fast enough. But the flies in Pibor are another matter—relentless, maddening, merciless, eternally landing on your sweaty hands and arms and cheeks and nose, on the goat meat being butchered nearby, on your water bottle. Swat one and four more seem to arrive in response—until about 7:30 p.m. when, as if by magic, they simply disappear.

Osman is a local kid and doesn't seem bothered by the flies or the heat. Maybe that's because this life beats the one he was living when he carried an assault rifle and served as a bodyguard for a high-ranking officer. It was a typical job for a child soldier in the Cobra faction. Korok, a baby-faced 16-year-old from Pibor, tells me he did the same thing during his two years of service. "They gave me a gun," he says as his large, lively eyes dart about. "I followed big men around."

After his father was shot and killed and his mother died of malaria, Korok found himself alone. His brother was off serving in the SPLA when soldiers from that force rampaged through the area around Pibor, punishing the local population—men, women, and children of the Murle tribe—for an uprising by native son and recurrent rebel David Yau Yau.[95]

A former theology student, Yau Yau once served as the Pibor county secretary of the South Sudan Relief and Rehabilitation Commission, a federal agency devoted to the reintegration and resettlement of refugees and internally displaced people.[96] He has, however, spent the last five years forging a career out of anti-government uprisings. A young upstart from the Murle minority, Yau Yau bucked local elders and ran for parliament as an independent in April 2010. After losing—he was reportedly trounced—Yau Yau pursued another path to power, this time through an armed rebellion with 200 fighters under his command. Just over a year later, after some skirmishes with government forces and minor acts of banditry, he accepted an offer of amnesty and was reportedly made a general in the SPLA.[97]

In March 2012, the SPLA launched a "disarmament campaign" in Murle areas around Pibor marked, locals say, by rampant atrocities, including rapes and assaults. Soon, Yau Yau was again in revolt, attracting boys like Korok and Osman to his South Sudan Democratic Movement/Army, also known as the SSDM/A-Cobra faction. That August, with thousands flocking to his cause and armed with heavier weapons, he launched his first major attack, an ambush that, according to the Small Arms Survey, killed more than 100 SPLA soldiers. Battles between the two forces raged through 2013 while civilians around Pibor continued to suffer. SPLA court-martial documents I obtained attest to the violence in the area: on July 31, 2013, Sergeant Ngor Mayik Magol and Private Bona Atem Akot shot and killed two Murle women and injured a child in Pibor County. Tried and convicted, they were ordered to pay "blood compensation" of 45 cows for each woman, sentenced to five years in prison, and fined 2,000 South Sudanese pounds each. In fact, according to Human Rights Watch, 74 Murle civilians, 17 of them women and children, were killed between December 2012 and July 2013.

In May 2014, several months after a full-fledged civil war erupted in South Sudan, Kiir and Yau Yau agreed to a peace pact.[98] Later, the former rebel leader pledged to demobilize the children among his forces.

In January 2015, the Cobra faction did indeed begin releasing youths, ages 9 to 17, some of whom had been fighting for up to four years.[99] In an initial demobilization ceremony, overseen by the South Sudan National Disarmament, Demobilization, and Reintegration Commission with support from UNICEF, 280 youngsters turned in their weapons and uniforms.[100] Since then, almost 1,500 others have been released.[101] "These children have been forced to do and see things no child should ever experience," said UNICEF South Sudan Representative Jonathan Veitch.[102] "The release of thousands of children requires a massive response to provide the support and protection these children need to begin rebuilding their lives."

Zuagin tells me he's 15, but he looks a couple years younger. His legs seem to be hiding somewhere inside his pants and his shirt is a size too big. Hailing from the nearby town of Gumuruk, he had served with the Cobra faction for about two years before being demobilized in February 2015. Like the other boys, he now spends his days at "the ICC" or Interim Care Center in Pibor, a compound dominated by a mud-walled church with a crude likeness of Christ drawn on an exterior wall.

"UNICEF builds and runs the centers with our partners—they are providing temporary care and shelter to the children released while we trace their families," UNICEF's Claire McKeever explains to me. "We have also trained local teams of social workers, cooks, and guards who work at the centers. The children are provided with food, shelter, items like mosquito nets, mats, and soap, psychosocial support and recreation activities. This is a two-year program in Pibor, but the hope is that these centers can become youth centers once the last children return home."

The child veterans at the ICC are like kids anywhere. Some are curious but apprehensive, others wary and insecure; a few of the older ones act tougher and cooler than they are. They find themselves on either side of that ethereal adolescent dividing line—some with the softer, rounder faces of little boys, others beginning to sport the more angular features of young men; some with tiny, falsetto voices, others speaking in tenor tones. As a group, they are, however, united by body type: uniformly skinny, swimming in their button-down shirts or soccer jerseys. Quite a few sport generic t-shirts emblazoned with the name "Obama." Many have energy to burn and a hunger for something more. A number of them seem to delight in tormenting one of their caretakers, a man who wields a long thin branch that he brandishes in an attempt to keep the boys in line. He threatens them with it, swinging it at them, though without much chance of actually hitting the speedy young veterans. They, in turn, mock him and when he sets his switch down, they steal it from him. He tells me that he likes the boys, that they are good kids. He also asks if I could help him get any other kind of job, anything at all.

Zuagin was yet another Cobra faction bodyguard who had spent his tour of duty toting a gun to protect an older man with a high rank. "He treated me well, with respect," he says, but assures me that life is now much better than it was with the militia. He has big plans for the future. "I want to go to school," he explains. "I want to be a doctor. We need sanitation. If I'm a doctor, I can help the community."

Zuagin has a ready solution to South Sudan's bloodshed. "To stop the violence, we need disarmament. All the guns need to be collected. After that, all the youths should go to school." I listen and nod, thinking about how a disarmament campaign led directly to violence here in Pibor, the very violence that Osman tells me cost his father his life and that forced so many of Zuagin's fellow child soldiers into the arms of the Cobra faction in the first place. I decide not to mention it.

Osman has his own simple solution: full employment. "To have peace, they should give a job to everybody," he says in a soft, raspy voice. "If they gave work to everybody, everybody would be busy and there would be no time for fighting."

Like the rest of the boys, Peter looks younger than the age he gives, which is 16. And like many of the others, it was abuse by the SPLA that, two years earlier, led him to flee his home and join the Cobra faction. "They were beating people. They even stole my clothes," he tells me as we sit in the minimal shade of a tree near the church in the ICC compound. Life with the militia was tough: cooking, chores, bodyguard duties, combat. Now, the bright-eyed youth says, he has free time and his life is so much better. He was looking forward to school, too, but didn't have the requisite 20 South Sudanese pounds needed for tuition. It's the same story for Osman who longs for school, but says he lacks the funds to attend.

"Getting all children in Pibor back to school is a priority and services are slowly being reestablished after many years of under-investment," UNICEF's McKeever tells me by email. "There are currently close to 3,000 children enrolled in Pibor [and nearby]

Gumuruk and Lekuangule and one in three of the demobilized children from Pibor are in accelerated learning programs."

The Interim Care Center is a spartan facility by Western standards. Creature comforts are few, but these young Cobra faction veterans have it better than many of their peers who find themselves hungry, malnourished, displaced, homeless, hopeless.[103] "Life is very good here," Osman tells me, praising the freedom to come and go as he pleases and wear civilian clothes. "Plus, I'm eating for free," he adds. When I ask if he ever wants to be a soldier again, he shoots me a disgusted look, before cracking a big smile and laughing aloud. "No. I don't like it at all. The worst part was fighting."

Zuagin, who speaks some English, agrees. In a tiny voice that has yet to crack, let alone deepen, he swears that life now is so much better than when he carried a weapon and that he's absolutely done with soldiering forever. All the boys I talk to assure me of the same thing—though it's no guarantee that some of them won't end up back under arms in the years to come. Above all, however, every one of them wants something more. All are looking for some way out.

Peter bluntly requests that I take a couple of the boys back to the United States so they can tell their stories in person. He strongly hints that he would like to be one of them. In the meantime, he says, he will "pray for peace." Korok, it turns out, is praying too—for peace and better leadership for the country. "Is there a possibility," he asks, "for the American people to set up schools, so the children could go to class instead of becoming soldiers?"

"South Sudan needs development. It needs hospitals, not fighting," Zuagin tells me with a thoughtful smile. True enough, but I wonder if there is any chance of it happening.

At the end of our interview, Zuagin stares into my eyes, squinting as if looking for something, and then begins interviewing me. What am I up to, he wants to know. Why have I traveled all this way to the ICC to talk to the other boys and him?

I try to explain how my country helped facilitate the recruitment of child soldiers in his, despite international condemnation of the practice and the fact that one of our laws forbids it, as does South Sudanese law.[104] But year after year, President Obama provided waivers to sidestep the 2008 Child Soldiers Prevention Act, by which Congress prohibited the U.S. from providing military assistance to governments filling out their ranks with children.[105] I say that people in America know little or nothing about the global scourge of child soldiers. It's important, I add, that they hear what boys like him have to say.

I had come, I explain, to hear his story and will do my best to tell it. I can feel Zuagin's disappointment. Like a number of the children, he clearly hoped for more from me—maybe even tangible assistance of some sort. He manages to look skeptical and remain silent until we reach the outer edge of awkward. Then, suddenly, he breaks into a wide grin and gracefully lets me off the hook.

Clearly, U.S. assistance and nation-building efforts in South Sudan have had anything but the desired effects either for Washington or South Sudan.[106] No less clearly, President Obama's gamble that looking the other way when it came to child soldiers would, in the long run, facilitate the end of their use imploded in 2013 with devastating results.[107] Despite this, Zuagin refuses to sour on the United States or at least its citizens. Somehow, in spite of all the disappointments, including me, he continues to have faith.

"I'm happy to have talked with you," he says with a nod, still smiling as we sit in the fading afternoon sun at this parched, uncertain way station, a literal no-man's-land located somewhere between war and peace, youth and adulthood. "If the American people read about us, maybe it will lead to something good."

◆

While I was reporting in South Sudan, *What's In Blue*, a United Nations Security Council report, announced an upcoming briefing on the U.N. Mission in South Sudan that was to be followed by "consultations." Assistant Secretary-General for Human Rights Ivan Simonovic, it said, might even raise the issue of "UNMISS's investigations into allegations that large-scale human rights [violations] have been committed in South Sudan." If he did, however, it would probably happen in hushed tones behind closed doors, given, as *What's In Blue* put it, "the sensitive nature of the issue."[108]

Few outside the country, it seems, are particularly eager to speak openly and honestly about the atrocities that occurred here. Only days before, the African Union had decided not to release a long-awaited report on the human rights abuses committed during the crisis. This prompted an outcry from groups like Amnesty International and Human Rights Watch, leading to swift denunciations of "so-called human rights organizations" by South Sudan's Information Minister Michael Makuei. "We will first bring peace and thereafter make people accountable," he added. "You cannot put the cart before the horse."[109]

Edmund Yakani, the man I asked about the location of mass graves over a beer, doesn't buy it. A lawyer by training, he cut his teeth investigating atrocities in Sudan's troubled Darfur region as a rule of law officer for the United Nations Development Program. Now, he's a full-time human rights activist, a leading member of what is, presently, a very small group of volunteers and activists attempting to press for accountability in South Sudan, regardless of ethnicity or tribe. He believes that mindsets like Makuei's are beyond dangerous. "This argument—peace first, justice later—doesn't work. Peace is a result of justice. When justice prevails, then you can have peace. But this argument that justice will come later, that doesn't work in an African context."

Revenge, he insists, is inevitable if there's no accountability. Without that, a cycle of violence will continue to churn, destroying lives and nurturing future conflict. "Those responsible for all these atrocities must be held accountable. Why? Because in 1991, no one was held accountable for those atrocities and look what happened. In fact, those responsible were sent back to the center of power. The government is now full of perpetrators that we know have committed atrocities. We can't compromise on these issues again."[110]

But who has the power to bring the "big men," the political leaders and military commanders, to justice? Who has the power to hold men with guns accountable for their crimes? To talk to just such a man, I travel to a spot in the outskirts of Juba where the road widens, the traffic thins, and military uniforms begin to outnumber civilian garb. I gaze out the window at a completely empty road that splits off from the main drag. It leads to an imposing entrance to a sprawling compound. This, I'm told, is the Presidential Gate, the one that Salva Kiir himself uses on his weekly visits. "Every Thursday, *every* Thursday, the president visits *them!* Have you ever heard of that?" a former advisor to the SPLA asked me. "Have you ever heard of a president visiting his army every Thursday?"[111]

I'm driven to a different gate, step out of the car, and wade into a sea of military men—and a few military women—streaming into the SPLA's General Headquarters at Bilpam. Though I stand out like a sore thumb, nobody pays any attention to me until I reach the main gate where a soldier directs me to two officers seated at a card table. One of them half-heartedly glances at the passport I thrust at him. "I'm here to see Brigadier General Henry

Oyay Nyago," I say. He gives no flicker of recognition. Knowing that I regularly mangle local names, I pull out a piece of paper with the general's name on it, and show it to him. Same result, but this time he rouses himself and leads me just inside the walls of the massive compound and through the green metal door of a concrete guardhouse. I find myself in a cramped bunker with a couple of desks. Three men in uniform are seated behind one of them. I take note of the open can of malt liquor on the desktop.

My escort points me toward them and I dutifully go through the same routine: passport, General Henry Oyay Nyago, piece of paper. The man in the middle says, "You call him." I pull out my phone, dial a number, and cross my fingers. Nyago has multiple phones and phone numbers. Sometimes when I call, it simply rings and rings unanswered. It can go on for hours. This time, however, I hear his rumbling baritone voice in seconds. He gently chastises me for not following his instructions to go to the main gate where there is paperwork with my name. I tell him I'm at the main gate, but they won't let me through. I don't quite catch his reply.

"You're sending someone?" I ask. I'm unsure whether he says yes before hanging up, but nonetheless turn to the man at the desk and say with confidence, "He's sending someone." He looks as if he couldn't care less. After another moment's awkwardness, I'm ushered to a metal chair with a blue seat cushion.

I scan the room, taking note of the phone numbers scrawled on the concrete walls, a large rock that might be deployed to prop the door open, a yellow plastic jerry can of the type ordinarily used to store and cart water, and the old-time ledger books that sit atop piles of dusty paperwork on the main desk. The little bunker is a hive of activity—buzzing cell phone ring tones, animated conversation, and loads of laughter. I sit anxiously amid the cacophony.

Officers come in, prompting salutes all around. I'm an oddity, a wayward *khawaja*—the Sudanese-Arabic term for a white person—stranded on their base. Each of them shakes my hand and gives me a big smile and a hearty hello. Each time I think it might be the man sent to retrieve me. Each time, I'm wrong. After the first 10 minutes, I give up wondering and settle back to watch the show out the door, the endless parade of soldiers walking through the main gate in every imaginable kind of SPLA uniform. Most are unarmed, but every so often a young man walks in toting a weapon, an AK-47 or sometimes a machine gun.

Finally, an officer arrives with paperwork, which he hands to one of the men at the desk, who looks over at me and says, "You Nick?" When I respond in the affirmative, he indicates that I should follow the young officer. No further ID is needed.

I'm led into the sprawling base dotted with nondescript white and cream-colored buildings that have nothing of the military about them. Camouflage Toyota pickups and olive-drab buses roll by. Men in uniforms of all sorts pass us wearing green berets and red berets and even, in one case, an olive boonie hat. On my way, I'm introduced to a man in olive drab with desert-colored boots. One arm is in a makeshift sling. "He was shot in the crisis of 2013," my escort, a captain, tells me. The man points to his right shoulder with his left hand, grimaces, then breaks into a smile and shakes my hand using his good arm.

The grounds are mostly cocoa-colored dirt and gravel well sprinkled with blue plastic water bottle caps. The shrubbery is tastefully manicured. Civilian-looking vehicles are parked under carports, including a white van with a blue stripe and "Staff" painted on its nose. A sign across the top of the windshield says "God is First."

In the heart of the base in the middle of a paved roundabout is a giant statue of John Garang clad in camouflage fatigues and combat boots, an assault rifle strapped to his back. We walk on further until I'm ushered into one of the cream-colored buildings. A thin wall partially divides its single long corridor. The floor is pitted, painted concrete. I'm ushered past a couple doors and into an office with a gray refrigerator, a black couch, and a coffee table. Brigadier General Henry Oyay Nyago is sitting behind a gigantic desk. To his left is an immense china cabinet-cum-bookshelf. The scale of the furniture befits the man. About 7 feet tall, he would be a commanding presence even without the three stars in a triangular pattern beneath an eagle on each shoulder. As he rises to greet me, he seems to unfurl upward and outward.

The Judge Advocate General and Director of Military Justice, Nyago is the top man went it comes to prosecuting soldiers who have committed crimes. So who better to speak to about the issue of SPLA atrocities? "Did you investigate cases of human rights abuses during the crisis?" I soon ask.

"No," he responds in his deep voice. I cock my head, waiting for more. He relents. "The president gave the order for former judges to investigate human rights abuses during the crisis," he finally says, referring to the "Investigation Committee to Investigate on Human Rights Abuses in the Attempted Coup of 15th December 2013," a panel formed at Kiir's behest in 2014 and headed by former chief justice John Wol Makec.[112] "If there was a case and we found evidence, we would send it to that panel," he adds.

As it happens, on his immense desk lay a conspicuous array of human rights-ish materials, including the 2008 edition of the U.S. military's Manual for Courts-Martial, a 1995 edition of Linda Malone's *International Law*, and a branded clock provided by the International Committee of the Red Cross. I take it all in and ask the next logical question: "Did you discover cases that you turned over to the committee?"

"No," he replies, and promptly launches us in other directions through a hail of scattershot words.

Nyago is a cipher. At least, he presents himself that way, but he's in a tough spot. He's an outsider, a Shilluk among Dinkas and a former officer in Sudan's armed forces. Now, he wears the insignia of the SPLA on an all-olive uniform: shirt, belt, and pants that are tucked into his desert-colored boots. His hair is clipped short and dark-rimmed glasses give him a scholarly appearance. Getting nowhere with questions about justice and impunity, I ask if he was nonplused about having investigations taken out of his hands by the president, but nothing there either. When I ask for some statistics on military crimes in this period, he reaches for a sparse binder in his imposing cabinet and begins to show me spreadsheets and data on the subject of military discipline. He flips to one page concerning 2014 general courts-martial. I crane my neck to get a closer look. The page lists 63 criminal cases, 51 cases of "military nature," four appeal cases, two civil cases, and one traffic case. Cases of a military nature, he tells me, are offenses like desertion and losing one's rifle. I inquire about the neutrally worded category "criminal cases." "These are…?" I ask.

"Murder," he replies. All 63, he says, are incidents in which soldiers killed civilians or fellow soldiers and represent all such proceedings involving the SPLA in 2014. Seventeen of the cases, according to the documents, had been tried as of October of that year, while 29 were still pending.

Nyago then turns to the subject of the training his forces received from the United States. He recalls traveling there and meeting with James Baker, the chief judge of the U.S. Court of Appeals for the Armed Forces. He tells me that the U.S., as well as the U.N., cut off all training after the crisis began without explanation. "They never told me a reason, they just said a mandate came down," he recalls. (A U.S. State Department official assures me that embassy personnel actually explained the situation to a number of higher-ranking generals, including Nyago's direct superior, Lieutenant General Malual Ayom Dor, in person. "They were responsible for informing their subordinates," she tells me by email. The United Nations says they did meet with Nyago. "On his return to Juba… UNMISS met with him at the Yam hotel in February 2014 where he was informed of the U.N. decision to suspend all activities," a spokesman informs me.)[113]

I also question Nyago about his experience during the 2013 crisis, as I had been told that he might have had some inkling of what was coming. "I was not here for it," he replies.

"Did you know something was going to happen?"

He shakes his head.

"You just happened to leave right before it?" I ask with some skepticism.

He then launches into a confusing story about an earlier leave of his having been postponed and notes that "Danny," an American advisor, kept him informed about the fighting in Juba while he was away. This, I assume to be a reference to Dan Lizzul, a longtime U.S. military justice advisor to the SPLA. I contact Lizzul and he seems open to talking, but the State Department denies me the right to speak with him. "Mr. Lizzul was not in South Sudan at that time," a State Department official tells me when I ask about his interactions with Nyago, "but it would have been quite normal for them to remain in some contact in those weeks."[114]

His family, Nyago points out, was still at home in Jebel Market when the fighting broke out.

"So were you worried?" I ask.

"No, I wasn't worried," he replies.

"Even with your family here?"

"No. I was in touch with them and then they went to Khartoum [the capital of Sudan]." I stare at him quizzically. "There's no reason to worry. There's nothing you can do."

According to Nyago, he didn't return to Juba until January 2014. I ask how it looked to him. "It was normal," he responds. When I continue to prod him about all the untended human rights abuses of those months, he begins to show annoyance for the first time. "You know," he finally says, "you should go talk to the former chief justice. He's the one who knows about these cases." Then he reiterates that he had nothing to do with any investigations of abuses during the crisis and our interview is clearly at an end.[115]

From this, the conclusion is clear enough. If General Nyago can't deal with the slaughter and abuses of every sort that set off the present civil war, who will? I ask a well-placed U.N. source about how the impunity of the security forces can be checked and he offers what he considers the sole possible prescription: "The SPLA needs to be disbanded and, on creation of a new constitution, there needs to be the creation of a new national army with… new structures, new training, new selection. You cannot have an army when the people in that army still identify strongly with their tribal background rather than the army background. That needs to be broken. And the only way that you can break that is to reinvent them as a new army, under a new constitution, in a new uniform, with a new name."

That, I point out, would mean a wholesale housecleaning of the top brass. "They should be transferred directly to The Hague for trial, the entire top structure," he replies.

"Most of the police, the security forces here [in Juba] come from just one tribe, the tribe of the president, almost 75 percent to 80 percent," confides a civil servant whose tribe is neither Dinka nor Nuer, a man with an intimate knowledge of the hardships of the long struggle for independence and the atrocities of the more recent crisis. "If you're all from one tribe and if one of you commits a crime, others will condone this. It's one of the biggest problems."

There used to be many Nuer in the security forces, he notes, but since the outbreak of violence in 2013, Dinkas have dominated. "It's a very dangerous situation. This is actually a first step toward genocide. If you look at the path toward genocide, this is how it begins—people talking about 'we' and 'you.' Once you divide yourselves into groups, once you see the security apparatus leaning toward one tribe, it's very, very dangerous. Anything can now happen at any time."

And it's true that today tribalism and the urge for revenge loom over everything in South Sudan. U.N. officials speak endlessly of the dynamics of tribalism. Many South Sudanese talk about revenge in the abstract before moving on to safer territory by mentioning peace, justice, and the International Criminal Court. Gatluak Tot isn't one of them. Tot says he's 38 but looks older—like a man who has seen a lot, too much actually. When you talk with him, you have the eerie feeling that's he's looking through, not at, you. What hair he still has is longer than the usual style here for men, as is his beard. A Nuer serving in the SPLA, he was on leave in Juba when the crisis exploded. He hid out for a month, some of that time in the bush on the outskirts of the capital, before finding safe haven at a U.N. camp. He believes that he escaped imminent execution at the hands of Dinka policemen and ever since, he has been collecting videos and photos on his phone. Using precious money, memory, and time, he's been assembling a digital library of horrors—videos of dead bodies and of corpses being abused and kicked into mass graves, as well as a range of grisly photos of massacre victims—all of them, video or still, are ghastly images.

I've seen some of these before. Online, you can find all sorts of footage and photos of purported atrocities in South Sudan. Other interviewees have pulled out their phones and shown me various kinds of "evidence" of what civil war means in this country. Some images are undoubtedly real; some are almost certainly fakes or photos of atrocities from other places. Different men keep them for different reasons. Gatluak Tot preserves them to stoke his sense of vengeance.

"I keep these to refresh the horror, the anger, in my mind. I watch them so I don't forget what the government did," he says, eyes bloodshot and blank. I take special note of his black polo shirt. On the right shoulder is the line "Team Glock Shooting Club, Safariland Surefire" and an image of a pistol lies over his heart. I ask Tot how often he views these videos and images. "At least twice a week. It refreshes my memory. It takes my mind back. It doesn't take me long to recall what the government did." He thrusts his worn red flip phone toward me. I shield the tiny screen from the unrelenting sun, but I can't see a thing and hand it back. He reloads the image and leans close. "This is from Guedele 1," he says, showing me a photo of what appear to be scores, maybe 50 to 75 corpses filling the frame. I've never seen this image before and have no idea if it's really from Guedele, but to Gatluak Tot it's undoubtedly, unquestionably real—as real as his rage.

Tot doesn't want a peace deal. He doesn't want Kiir to step down. He makes a special point of telling me that he doesn't want the president tried before the ICC. He is also adamantly against assassination. He won't be satisfied until Kiir is ousted by force of arms. He wants him to experience the defeat of his forces, to watch his power crumble, to see the consequences of his actions. Tot wants to be a part of this military campaign. He sees it as his chance for revenge. His eyes light up at the prospect. It's the only time they show life during our conversation.

All Tot asks for is a fair fight. Almost every Nuer I speak to is convinced that, in addition to the Ugandan troops that bolster Kiir's forces, there is a pan-African force supporting him whose makeup changes depending on the interviewee, but usually includes soldiers from Egypt, Ethiopia, Kenya, Nigeria, Rwanda, Somalia, Sudan, or Libya. (No one pays the slightest attention when I mention that Libya is a near-failed state with no army to deploy.) Without his foreign allies, Tot is convinced, Kiir would fall fast. Two days, no more, he says, though you can sense that he would like it to take longer—time enough for sufficient payback. "I want revenge," he tells me again and again. I ask if he means to direct his vengeance at Kiir's military or all Dinkas. "Any of the two," he says in a voice as rough as sandpaper.

"So what happens if you're successful and oust Kiir?" I ask.

"Then I can forgive," he replies and vows to forgo further acts of vengeance. After Kiir's fall, he insists, Machar will build roads and schools and foster economic development. Wait, I say. Do you want elections or will Machar just take over? Yes, elections are good, he tells me, though he can't conceive of a scenario in which his candidate won't win. I'm just about to ask him how the cycle of violence will ever end if the military campaign he envisions lumps Dinka civilians with military combatants when he launches into a monologue on how Nuer culture doesn't allow either killing based on ethnicity or of those not involved in the fighting. Somehow, I feel defeated and don't see a point in dragging this out. Instead, I thank him for his time and watch him slowly walk away, wondering how long before he fires up his phone and immerses himself once again in his digital museum of horrors.

◆

Horror shows are plentiful in a country at war, but some are grimmer than others. Bentiu, a mostly Nuer town and the capital of Unity State, fell into rebel hands on December 21, 2013, when the local military commander defected to Machar's forces. As in Bor, armed Nuers promptly launched attacks meant as reprisals for the killings in Juba. Joseph Monytueil, the governor of Unity State, told Human Rights Watch that 70 civilians were killed in Bentiu in those early days. On January 10, the rebels abandoned the town as fighters from the Justice and Equality Movement or JEM, a Sudanese rebel group, and SPLA forces advanced.[116] At that time, as many as 2,000 Dinkas who had taken shelter at a nearby U.N. base climbed its fence, joined those forces, and began attacking civilians on the outskirts of the compound, kicking off a new round of mayhem and violence.

Now, it was Nuer civilians who fled to the U.N. base. According to witnesses, at least 31 were killed as they ran or when they failed language tests. Their bodies were scattered on the road between the town and the site. U.N. human rights officers watched as SPLA forces shot at civilians right outside their base, killing one man. Another time, they saw soldiers stop a car heading to the site and gun down the passengers as they ran.[117] Other Nuers fled into swampland where SPLA troops hunted them down.[118] Still others were killed in Bentiu, which was soon in flames as the marketplaces on either side of the main road went up in smoke. U.N. satellite imagery later showed that almost 1,200 buildings—about 8 percent of the town—had been destroyed. Rubkona, a nearby rebel-held town sacked by SPLA and JEM forces, fared even worse. There, nearly 4,000 structures, most of the town, was destroyed.[119]

Sheldon Wardwell, the American aid worker with the long blond locks, was dropped into this tornado of devastation on January 12 when the country director of the tiny NGO he worked for, Nonviolent Peaceforce (NP), dispatched him to Bentiu as part of a four-person team, some of the first humanitarians to return to the ravaged region. After landing on the airstrip just south of the Protection of Civilians (POC) site, he and three coworkers—including a fellow Californian and NP's Bentiu team leader Calista Pearce—caught a ride back to the U.N. base. "On the way," Wardwell recalls, "I saw—in the distance—a bird eating a body on the road. One of those giant cranes."

There were still corpses strewn about and, in the months ahead, as the town repeatedly changed hands, Wardwell would come across similar scenes again and again. "Over my nine months in Bentiu," he tells me, "I saw the roads get cleaned up of bodies and I saw them littered with bodies on a number of different occasions. I've seen literally hundreds of bodies in Bentiu and Rubkona after a series of battles."

The situation inside the U.N. base was appalling. Adequate food, water, and shelter were lacking. Children were dying, sometimes almost daily, he tells me. One of NP's jobs was to accompany grieving, wailing mothers outside the safety of the compound to bury the tiny bodies of their children.[120] "Seeing a bunch of dead bodies when you're driving by in a vehicle is one thing," Wardwell confides. "But seeing these mothers completely broken down was probably one of the most difficult things. I had never seen anything like this—not even close. It quickly became the norm, though... Most of the time we just drank a lot, which doesn't help at all, I learned."

In April, rumors began circulating that the rebels were preparing to mount a new assault on Bentiu. On the morning of the January 14, civilians began fleeing from Torabeit, about 50 kilometers north of Bentiu. But when one group of civilians seeking sanctuary at the POC site were turned back at a government checkpoint, they found themselves stranded in the path of two armies, one angry and in retreat, the other on the march and out for revenge.[121]

As the government forces fell back, the JEM irregulars established a defensive line about a mile south of the U.N. base. Just south of them were SPLA troops, while from the north the rebels were closing in fast. Between them was, of course, the base where Wardwell received some disturbing news reminiscent of his experience with the naked man in Juba but on an exponentially larger scale.

"We just got information that about 60 women and children were at the airstrip two miles south of our location," he recalls. "So, if you can imagine, to the north of us within eight kilometers, we have opposition forces coming in our direction and then to the south of us one kilometer is the [government's] front line and one kilometer beyond that is the airstrip… and then beyond that, there's another checkpoint. So you know that the women and children that are stuck at this airstrip are not able to go right and they're not able to go left—and there's a looming attack at any moment. And these people are going to be trapped right in the middle of it." The only question was when.

"So I go to speak with the U.N. liaison officer and ask him what are they going to do to extract the civilians and they say nobody's moving outside the base at all because they're bracing for an attack… which is reasonable," Wardwell tells me. After all, he points out, the U.N. had tens of thousands of lives to safeguard at the POC site. "At the same time, I look at the situation and I know there are 60 women and children stuck two kilometers away and… they're 100 percent going to be caught in the middle."

Pearce tells me that the distance to the airport and the number of people there suggested they could pull off the rescue mission, but it wasn't as simple as just hopping in a Land Cruiser. There were protocols to follow, plans to make, and staff in Juba to contact. "We learned as much as we could, did a security analysis—which Sheldon was a little impatient with," she confides. "He's really gung-ho. Really passionate… There were times when he got really frustrated with me."

After they got the green light from NP, Pearce asked the other three NP staffers who would consider volunteering for such a mission. "It's all quiet," Wardwell recalls with a laugh. "So Calista says, 'As team leader, I'll go.'"

"I don't remember when I decided I would go," Pearce confesses, explaining that all NP operations are generally carried on a volunteer basis. "I sort of figured that I would go… At that point you know what your team's security thresholds are. I imagine that I had in mind that the others can do it if they want to, but probably only Sheldon will want to. So it would probably be me and him." Indeed, Wardwell tells me that he alone volunteered to join her.

It was between four and five o'clock, with rain beginning to fall, when Wardwell hopped behind the wheel of NP's white Land Cruiser with Pearce in the passenger seat. First, they visited the U.N. liaison officer to discuss their plan. If the United Nations wasn't going to save these people, Wardwell told him, then NP would. The official wasn't pleased, but there was no way for him to stop them.

The Land Cruiser, a spare tire lashed to the roof rack, was already slip-sliding in the slickening gray mud when it arrived at the camp's gate where Wardwell signed them out with the Mongolian guards. "Calista is saying a prayer," Wardwell recalls, "and just as we are pulling out of the gate she says—and Calista's quite experienced—'this is by far the most dangerous situation with NP that I've put myself in intentionally.'"

"I do remember texting my now-husband—at the time, he was in Juba—and saying 'Can you pray for us? We're heading out to do something risky,'" Pearce says when I ask her about this moment at the gate. "As we were leaving, I think Sheldon asked me if I was nervous and I was like 'Yeah, this is the riskiest thing I've ever intentionally set out to do with NP.' As the team leader, I probably shouldn't have said it," she admits.

"That's not exactly type of thing you want to hear, is it?" I say to Wardwell.

"I knew the danger of the situation. I wasn't just being reckless. We're talking about maybe 60 lives of women and children," he replies.

As they pulled through the gate Wardwell, still an NP neophyte, began to second-guess himself—if only momentarily. "Oh fuck. I'm the asshole who pushed for this and now I'm also putting Calista's life and my own in danger," he thought to himself.

I ask Pearce if she had felt pressured in any way. "Not at all," she replies without the slightest hesitation. "I knew he wanted to do it, but I wanted to do it, too... I really did want to do something to help these people." With that, the two Californians were off to run the gauntlet, hoping to outrace the rebel army bearing down on Bentiu.

"I pull out and we make a left-hand turn out of the base towards the south and right off the bat we're faced with two tanks and four technicals," Wardwell remembers, using the standard slang term for the war chariot of the developing world, the light pickup truck with a machine gun mounted in its bed. "It was a fucking sight, man."

Fearing that the government forces might mistake them for the rebels' lead element, Wardwell and Pearce thrust their arms out the windows. "I wanted to get my white-ass arm and head out the window, so that they can see it's somebody white coming toward them," he tells me, excitedly. Staring down the barrels of the tank main guns and machine guns, they rolled along the muddy, wrecked road toward the front line. "We went really slowly. We just tried to give them plenty of time to see that we were humanitarians," Pearce tells me. "It was definitely tense once we got out there. It was like 'I thought we had a plan.' But clearly there were some elements we didn't plan out." The plan, if you could call it that, was to stop at the checkpoints, let the soldiers know that they were from Nonviolent Peaceforce, that they were heading out to pick up some women and children, and that they'd be back shortly.

"I try to stop and it's these crazy-ass JEM guys who've just been in battle all morning and all afternoon and got their asses beat and they're clearly intoxicated. So as soon as I roll my window down to speak with them, they just want my ass out of their way," Wardwell recalls. After weaving through the tanks, trucks, and a mass of drunk soldiers and traveling a few hundred meters further, he arrives at the more orderly SPLA lines, where he informs the soldiers of their plans and then keeps heading south.

It doesn't take very long for Wardwell and Pearce to reach the airstrip, which is when they first spot the trapped civilians. A tiny girl wearing a peach dress with floral print sleeves, suitable for Easter Sunday. A boy in a brown t-shirt, jeans cut to shorts just below the knees. Young women in cotton print dresses, small children perched on their hips; others toting overstuffed rectangular bags, the type they might normally balance atop their heads. A small girl in a long purple dress with gray sleeves. A boy in a white button-down shirt and denim shorts. A toddler in a yellow top, another in a red shirt. Sixty women and children and four men, all of them now racing toward the Land Cruiser, swarming around it, grasping, desperate, frantic.

With the back gate open, Wardwell launches into crowd-control mode, explaining patiently that they will be making multiple trips and that the men will have to wait for a later run. "Calista and I jam-pack this Land Cruiser with 20 children and 7 women. They're literally crammed in like sardines," Wardwell recalls. "They were just packed from the floor to the ceiling—all women and children," echoes Pearce.

Getting that many people into the Toyota is an accomplishment in itself. They're ready to roll when those second thoughts rush up again. They have at least three round trips to go. Can they make them before the rebel attack begins? Or will they get caught in a no-man's-land of hostile fire between tanks and technicals, surging rebels and sullen, drunken militia? "Me and Calista were really feeling the heat," is the way Wardwell sums up the situation.

Nonetheless, he starts the engine, rolls on, and they do make it back and watch the women and children clamber out of the Land Cruiser to the safety of the POC site. Finally, Wardwell breathes his first sigh of relief. They've succeeded in saving 27 lives, but there's no time to rest or revel in that fact. It's back into the Toyota for a second shot at the gauntlet—and this time, their luck runs out. The increasingly wet, rutted road proves too much for the SUV. It founders in the muck.

Here, Wardwell and Pearce's recollections diverge and the fragile vagaries of human memory are thrown into broad relief. They both remember very specific overlapping details, but place and time have become jumbled with the amnesiac wash of adrenaline and the mind-clouding passage of time. I'm at a loss to say who is right.

"Oh my god," Wardwell remembers thinking to himself as he jumped from the Land Cruiser and kicked off his sandals. His toes sunk into the mud and so did his small shovel, but the SUV was stuck fast and going nowhere. Noticing their predicament, an SPLA soldier approached them, followed by others—one of them even getting behind the wheel as Wardwell begins to push. "I've never prayed so explicitly for an angel to come—and then the SPLA soldier came. I'm like, 'I think he was my angel. That is crazy,'" Pearce tells me with slight lilt in her voice.

Wardwell and the soldiers strained and shoved, muscles burning, and then, for some reason, the American turned his head and saw a completely unexpected sight. "As we're doing this, guess who shows up to the airstrip? A U.N. convoy with a big truck—an armed U.N. convoy!" Wardwell exclaims, his voice still dripping with incredulity almost a year later. The U.N. liaison officer had assured Wardwell that under no circumstances would they send personnel outside the wire with the rebels advancing. Yet here they were. Pearce insists that the U.N. vehicles were already at the airstrip when their Land Cruiser foundered on its mucky outskirts. Whatever the case, it seems clear to me that little NP had shamed the U.N. into action, but here all are in complete agreement—neither Wardwell, Pearce, nor U.N. officials will say anything of the sort.

With the U.N.'s assistance, all 64 people stranded at the airfield were safe at the UNMISS compound when rebel forces stormed into Bentiu the next morning. They survived, but many who fled elsewhere weren't so lucky. For them, there was no NP Land Cruiser, no U.N. convoy, no rescue.

Civilians seeking refuge at the Bentiu State Hospital were murdered en masse on April 15, 2014. "Under one building, they shot one Dinka and one Darfuri who were trying to escape," said a witness. "A group of at least 20 Darfuris were killed as they tried to escape out the back gate. There were also Nuers who were killed for being traitors." Médecins Sans Frontières reported that at least one healthcare worker and 27 people seeking shelter were slain there.[122]

Two days after their airport run, Pearce and Wardwell were part of another convoy that ventured out on a rescue mission. Carrying the cell phone numbers of desperate civilians who had made contact with family and friends in the POC site and were hiding out in various spots around Bentiu, they brought along a translator who could call the men and arrange to pick them up, Pearce tells me. It was a smart plan, but it all collapsed when the cell phone network did the same. The humanitarians were forced to go to the locations people had been in the days before. They saved some men—maybe 10 in all—but they often came up empty. The living were in short supply. The dead were a different story. "The town was completely destroyed. There were bodies everywhere," Wardwell recalls. "There were dead bodies lining the road. He was driving," Pearce says of Wardwell, "so I did a count. It was hard because some of them were piled up. As best as I could count—I counted 107 bodies." Wardwell adds, "That was just on the main road. We weren't canvasing the whole town… That was just what was visible on the roads that we went on."

Other bodies just disappeared. In the Kalibalek neighborhood, for instance, armed fighters killed civilians in the courtyard of a mosque. Other rebels barged into the mosque itself and opened fire. Still others executed a group of civilians near the minaret. More than 250 people were killed there. The bodies were loaded into a dump truck and driven away. A witness reported that 150 wounded were later transported to the hospital. When U.N. human rights officers arrived just days later, they discovered 185 shell casings, from both AK-47s and machine guns, scattered inside and outside the mosque. They also witnessed the removal of 37 corpses. Rebel leader Riek Machar acknowledged the killings in Bentiu and pledged to investigate.[123] There's little evidence to suggest he has.

Malakal, the capital of Upper Nile State, is another town that experienced widespread devastation, changing hands six times between December and April 2014. Civilians died in myriad ways, including those killed in the crossfire between the two armies and more than 200 who drowned when their boat capsized in the Nile. Both forces terrorized civilians with arbitrary arrests, armed robberies, and ethnically motivated killings.[124]

A 20-year-old Nuer man from Malakal told Human Rights Watch a typical tale of that moment: government troops detained two friends and him as they were trying to take refuge at the nearby U.N. compound. Tied up, they were handed over to a group of soldiers at a military barracks. "They lined us up outside of a building and started shooting at us," he recalled. All three were hit and both of his friends died. "When they shot at me, I just fell down," said the survivor. He lay there feigning death. An hour later, a soldier found him alive and took him to the hospital. He lost a hand. Other young Nuers were reportedly rounded up in a similar fashion and gunned down in cold blood.[125]

When rebel forces pushed into town, the hospital and churches became, as in Bor, sites for bloodbaths. "There were 11 dead bodies in the [Malakal Teaching] Hospital—patients murdered in their beds," an MSF emergency coordinator recalled. "We found three more bodies near one of the hospital gates."[126] Members of the Nuer White Army had burst in with guns, machetes, and spears, attacking people on the basis of their ethnicity, according to Human Rights Watch.[127] Patients said that armed men entered the hospital demanding money and cell phones. They assaulted everyone they could find and raped women and girls.

A 59-year-old man, injured during an attack on his house, had sought refuge at the hospital. He found anything but. "Every day they came: 10 to 15 armed men. And when they came, they would shoot. They demanded mobiles [cell phones] and money. If you didn't give them away, they would shoot you… In our ward, many people were shot. They beat all of us—old men, young men, young girls… They even took some girls and women away."[128] An MSF nurse reported: "There were corpses lying on the beds, and medicines, clothes, and suitcases scattered on the floor—a sign of the terror experienced by those who fled. We even found a patient hiding on the roof."[129]

By January 18, more than 4,000 people had reportedly sought refuge on the grounds of Malakal's Presbyterian church. About two days later, a pastor there was reportedly shot and killed by an SPLA soldier. A month after that, members of the White Army came to the church and, according to a witness, opened fire, killing around 30 people, most of them Shilluks.[130]

Elena Balatti, a sister from the Order of Comboni Missionaries who also manages a branch of the Catholic Radio Network in the area, published an account of what she witnessed in Malakal on Gurtong, a website that bills itself as an independent, not-for-profit, community-based "peace and media project." She wrote:

> At 6 p.m. [on February 18]… about 30 gunmen gathered in front of [Saint Joseph's Catholic] Cathedral. The Nuer men and the Murle pastor started talking to them. I joined the

group thinking to ask for a form of protection for the civilians... The leader of the group, talking in English, said... that they had come to look for 'somebody called Olony' inside the church. Olony, the leader of the Shilluk forces that were fighting alongside with the Government was surely not in St. Joseph's Cathedral. Nevertheless, one of the armed men cocked an RPG launcher and threatened to hit the church. After other negotiations, some elements of the White Army went inside and checked the people. Eventually they departed...

On Thursday 20, an appeal came to the UNMISS to rescue... 1,500 IDPs [internally displaced people] at Christ the King Catholic Church. I accompanied the afternoon patrol. Outside the gate of the church there were three bodies, seemingly civilians, and, immediately inside, the area that had been a workshop for carpentry and mechanics for more than 30 years was only a heap of ashes and contorted iron sheets still smoldering. When the people saw the U.N. vehicles they rushed towards us. It was as if they had seen a ray of hope and they requested to be helped to reach the UNMISS compound. They narrated how they had been harassed by the White Army. Shooting and killing had taken place within the church premises...

On Wednesday the 26, a group of people from Christ the King Church rushed to the UNMISS. Even old women... pushed themselves ahead on the long and dusty road. In the night, the rebel soldiers had taken away 9 girls. A few had come back in the morning after having been raped. One of them was 12 years old. There was no longer any kind of security even at Christ the King Church.[131]

As in Juba, Bor, and Bentiu, the UNMISS base in Malakal became a refuge for civilians escaping violence. By December 28, 2013, around 12,000 refugees were being sheltered there. A month later, that number had more than doubled.[132] Others took to the bush, ran for the river, or began long treks by road.

Veronica Ayang was one of them. She agrees to speak with me at her place of work in Juba. We find a quiet spot in the front office, a tiny room of once-white walls with a crackled, cratered, and chipped blue concrete floor. A few intriguing locked metal trunks with stencils of flowers and roosters on them line the edges of the room. I'm offered a seat in a plush scarlet easy chair adorned with velvet filigrees and partially covered by a large, ill-fitting piece of orange-dyed burlap. A fan is mounted to the wall, but looks like it hasn't run in years. Once in a while, a welcome breeze blows in from the open door that looks out onto a dirt road. At one point, I glance up just in time to see two small goats gently butting heads. Another time, I spy a sizeable lizard scaling the rear wall of a white-washed building across the road.

Twenty-six years old and a married mother of three, Ayang's eyes are bright. She sports short, straight hair with crimson highlights. She has pierced ears devoid of earrings. Her tall, slim body is sheathed in a heavy-looking gray business suit, a short-sleeved jacket over a long skirt. It's about 99 degrees and I wonder how she could possibly look so comfortable, sitting in a plastic chair, one leg tucked behind the other, while I'm sweeping sweat from my forehead.

Life was good before December 2013, she tells me in a soft, fluted voice. A member of the Shilluk ethnic group, she was married to a Dinka policeman and spent her days at home raising her children. "We were happy. We enjoyed life," she says, drawing her arms close to her body.

When Ayang first heard about the outbreak of fighting in Juba, it never occurred to her that it would travel north 520 kilometers to Malakal. But it did. As word came that the war was winding its way toward her home, she stockpiled two barrels of water along with extra flour and oil. The opposition forces captured the town on Christmas Day, prompting heavy exchanges of heavy firepower. Government soldiers retook the town on December 27. The opposition then had it from January 14th through the 19, before the government ousted them again.

Ayang didn't stay for all of that, but what she experienced was more than enough. The duties of her husband's job meant that he was involved in the battles for the town, leaving her alone with the children. As the fighting mainlined through the neighborhoods, Ayang stayed inside, spending much of her time under the bed with the children to minimize the possibility of being hit by gunfire or shrapnel.

Tired, frightened, and running out of food, she finally decided she had to make a break for it, so she and her kids joined a rush of locals fleeing their neighborhood. She hadn't gotten far before she saw a rebel soldier shoot a young man she knew. "We were all running out from our homes and they shot him down right in front of me," she says. Terrified, she ran back home with her children.

When the SPLA retook the town in late December, she tells me, they broke open all the shops in the market so that those like her who had ridden out the fighting and were now growing hungry could restock on essentials. She got provisions, then ran to the river to replenish her supplies of water. Things calmed briefly, but soon enough the fighting still going on outside the town started creeping ever closer.

As the combat intensified, Ayang decided to make a break for the river, but when she and the children got there, she realized that there was no way to get across. Her next thought was to head for the UNMISS POC site, where she was met by her husband. He soon returned home to see if he could salvage some of their belongings. He checked in on a neighbor, an elderly lady, and found her slain, she tells me.

With her husband still involved in the fighting for control of the town, Ayang and her children soon set off on the road for Fashoda, where, in 1898, the British famously checked French expansion into East Africa. Violence followed on her heels, but after two days of walking they arrived unscathed but with only the clothes on their backs. Luckily, relatives provided them with food and shelter. Three weeks into their stay in Fashoda, the Nuers began launching cattle raids in the area, beating women and killing some men, she says. Ayang was again filled with fear.

"On top of that," she tells me, "I'm married to a Dinka, my children are Dinka, so when my children are out playing and someone asks their name, they can be identified and they might be killed." So once again she took to the road, this time arriving in the town of Melut, where she was taken in by her uncles. From there, it was on to Palouch where her husband's brother bought her a plane ticket to fly to Juba, a city where she finally felt safe. Malakal, she tells me, is still too dangerous and she's afraid to go back.

"I was just trying to save my children," she says softly but emphatically. "As we moved from one place to the next, I was sure that things would calm down and the fighting would stop. After we went from Malakal to Fashoda, I thought it would be okay, but it wasn't. Then we went to Melut and I thought the fighting would stop, but it didn't. It never did… I didn't know if we would survive."[133]

No one knows how many of those who stayed in Malakal didn't survive. Between December 30 and January 3 alone, 218 bodies were buried in just one cemetery.[134] A South Sudan Red Cross volunteer told Human Rights Watch that local aid workers collected about 500 bodies in early January.[135]

U.N. satellite images of the town show shadowy smudges of loss—the charcoal-gray ghosts of what once were homes, shops, warehouses, whole neighborhoods that went up in flames. A count from a January 18 satellite photo offers a window onto the destruction: "515 residential and related structures" destroyed. Two months later, after government and rebel forces had each held the town for a month, the U.N. reported almost 9,900 residential structures and 204 businesses and warehouses destroyed. In all, about 22 percent of the town had disappeared.[136] By April 2014, more than 197,000 people had been driven from their homes in Upper Nile State and more than 19,000 civilians had sought protection in UNMISS POC sites in Malakal and Melut.

I arrived in Malakal a few months later, whisked there on a U.N. flight. It was the rainy season and it seemed that everything was sodden and soggy. The town was just creeping back to something resembling life and the U.N. base was a mud pit filled with dispirited, displaced people and overtaxed aid workers. I had to tie my heavy, green gumboots to my legs with wire to keep the gray muck from yanking them off. In that fashion, I slipped, slid, and slogged my way to the MSF hospital there.

The main ward was filled with victims from the terrible swirl of intermingled crises that added up to the cataclysm that was South Sudan: the baseline poverty and food insecurity that had already been part and parcel of daily life but had been intensified by the fighting and was now creeping toward famine; the lack of infrastructure and adequate medical care; the war itself. On 1 of 15 or so blue metal bed frames topped with thin mattresses, sullen mothers, and squalling children, I saw a tiny girl in a yellow top and pink skirt, her head dominated by a white bandage covered in a clingy mesh net. Nyajuma, just a year old, had arrived with her mother two weeks earlier, weighing only 11 pounds.

(According to the American Academy of Pediatrics, the average one-year-old girl in the U.S. weighs more than double that.) She was quickly started on the first of two powdered therapeutic foods to combat severe malnutrition, followed by a regimen of Plumpy'nut, a high-protein, high-calorie peanut paste, four times a day, along with two servings of milk.

But Nyajuma's problems went far beyond malnutrition. The bandages wrapped around her tiny head covered a skin infection. She also suffered from kala azar, a deadly disease caused by a parasite spread by sand flies that results in prolonged fever and weakness. On top of that, she was being treated for two other potentially lethal maladies, cholera and tuberculosis. Her mother, resting beside her, looked exhausted, broken, world-beaten. Pregnant on arrival, she gave birth five days later. She lay next to Nyajuma, listless, covering her face with her arm as if to shield herself from the world, though maybe it was only from my intruding eyes.

The hospital was filled with Nyajumas. About 10 percent of those arriving in her condition wouldn't survive, Javier Roldan, MSF's medical team leader told me. "We have people who come in in later stages or have a co-infection because malnutrition has compromised their immune system, which makes treatment much more complicated." He spoke of the difficulty of losing patients for want of better facilities, more staff, and greater resources. "The outcome of a baby weighing one and a half kilos [3.3 pounds] in Europe or America would be no problem at all, but here there's quite a high mortality rate," Roldan explained. "It's very frustrating for the medical staff when you have patients die because you don't have the means to treat them."

◆

The conflict in South Sudan is exacting a heavy toll on expat aid workers and not just the sort of psychological stress that pains the mind and poisons the soul. I think of this as my stomach sours from the relentless heat, a lack of food, and the overwhelming smell of aviation fuel mixed with the acrid funk of close to 20 sweating soldiers and policemen, all of us crammed aboard a Russian Mi-8 helicopter. We're seated against the outer walls with suitcases, rucksacks, cardboard boxes, and plastic coolers strapped down under a big cargo net in the center of this twin-engine chopper. The shadow of the blades chasing each other gives everything inside a shuddering, stop-motion quality. Over my shoulder, I peer out the window onto the treetops far below, my face suddenly in a cool stream of air from an open window.

I breathe in deeply as I scan the horizon, catching sight of another white U.N. helicopter far off and far below us. My mind drifts back to news reports from just a couple weeks after I had last been in-country. Rebel general Peter Gadet had alleged that these U.N. helos were being used to ferry the SPLA around the country and threatened to shoot them down. Less than 10 days later, near Bentiu, one of them was blasted out of the sky, killing three crewmembers and injuring a fourth.[137]

Those men, Russians all, were far from alone. The conflict is taking the life of about one humanitarian worker each month while I'm in-country. When I'm in Juba, a British employee of the U.S.-based Carter Center is executed in his organization's compound not far from my lodgings by an unidentified man with an AK-47. Some speculated it was a soldier with a grudge.[138] This, in a country with a great many soldiers with a great many grudges.

Another day, I'm sitting in the passenger seat of a car, traveling back from an interview in Juba when I cock my head and look up just as one of the ubiquitous SPLA camo pickup trucks slowly rolls past. A soldier sitting on the right wall of its bed is looking down at me. A red bandana is tied bandit-style across his face. His long, slender arms cradle an AK-47. A bare foot dangles down. We make eye-contact for a moment and then he's whisked off to who knows where to do who knows what. Another man in uniform in a country of men in uniforms: desert camouflage; olive green fatigues; plain tan fatigues; deep, forest-green fatigues; blue police camo; digital camo; orange camouflage; tiger-stripe camo; jungle and forest patterns. You name it and they've got it in South Sudan. Every kind of uniform: army, national police, local police, auxiliary police, wildlife service, national security, Ugandan military. Even the fire brigade wears camo. You see camo-clad men waiting at bus stops, seated on the backs of boda-bodas, piled into enormous transport trucks, leaning against formidable compound walls, lounging in parked gun trucks, crammed into technicals, sitting in plastic chairs in front of restaurants, talking on cell phones. You see them walking down dusty roads, automatic rifles strapped to their backs loosely enough to swing, two clips taped together for rapid reloading. Sometimes, men like these will drag a tree limb across a road to make you stop your car. Then they ask for a ride. Do you say no to an armed man on a dusty road in the middle of nowhere? What's the etiquette on that?

While I'm reporting there, South Sudan is in the midst of a clampdown on journalists "The number of journalists and reporters killed by security forces in war-torn South Sudan is growing as leaders are failing to halt violence," begins one story.[139] I run into frequent difficulties arranging interviews, coordinating travel, tracking down contacts. Though my own struggles pale in comparison to those of the local press, I do find myself thwarted and frustrated on a variety of fronts, including by my own country's government.

It's early one Saturday morning and the restaurant in my hotel is deserted—no diners, no waiters, just me, a few flies, and some blood-drunk mosquitoes oblivious to the breaking dawn. I spy a copy of the *Corporate*, which claims to be "South Sudan's Business Weekly," pick it up, meander over to a clean-ish table, brushing away a few crumbs, and check out the news. Despite the civil war, South Sudan's oil production has apparently risen by 9,000 barrels per day. The cost of food and nonalcoholic beverages is on the rise, too. American dollars are much in demand, South Sudanese pounds far less.

The newspaper's op-ed page is dominated by a piece headlined "South Sudan's Lessons from Dr. Martin Luther King, Jr.— Independence, Freedom, and Brotherhood." To be honest, I'm expecting the worst. And it begins in a distinctly Dr. King-lite style with an "I-Have-a-Dream" focus, heavy on "Christian beliefs," light on confrontation and militancy. But then the author moves on to a 1967 speech by the civil rights leader against the war in Vietnam. Included is a meaty excerpt highlighting America's "madness" and the "suffering poor" of Vietnam whose land was being "laid waste" and whose homes were being "destroyed." That, coupled with the op-ed author's plea for "accountability" in South Sudan and "justice for all, regardless of who they are" piqued my interest, especially since it turned out to be written by the U.S. ambassador to South Sudan.

I'm especially intrigued because Charles Twining knows the Vietnam War intimately. He served in the war zone as a young Foreign Service officer. Knowing something about the Vietnam War myself and what my country did there, knowing something about failures of American accountability, having spent more than 10 years, in fact, investigating U.S. atrocities that were rarely looked into at the time and often covered up for decades—I was eager to discuss these issues with America's ambassador.

I contact the embassy and ask for an interview. A few days later, a public affairs officer emails me for more information about just what I'm going to focus on. I immediately respond with details. He writes back for yet more information. Where exactly will the piece be published and in what form—print or online? I respond again and he goes silent. I follow up and, days later, he finally replies, asking how long I'll be in Juba. I let him know and he replies: "I'll get back to you this week with an answer." Monday, Tuesday, Wednesday, Thursday, Friday, Saturday, Sunday, Monday. I check in a number of times by phone and email. Nothing. That Tuesday, the better part of a month after my initial request, the public affairs officer emails me that the ambassador is aware of my request. "It is in his hands," I'm told, and I'll get a "yay or nay" from someone "soon."

Weeks, then months, pass and I never hear from the ambassador—but Edmund Yakani does. And for him, speaking with the U.S. ambassador is a much more pressing matter.

Yakani works out of a nondescript beige building with burgundy window frames tucked inside an ordinary-looking compound, itself folded into the anonymous jumble of Juba's unpaved streets not so far from the Kenyan embassy. Inside, it's a hive of activity for the men and women of the Community Empowerment for Progress Organization (CEPO) who work on a plethora of projects relating to human rights, gender-based violence, and the fostering of peace among South Sudan's diverse communities. Most of the office is a warren of small rooms with desks jammed end-to-end, maximizing nonexistent space. We sit in a much airier conference room and Yakani tells me about some of the many projects he's involved in. The particular one I've come to talk with him about is an orphaned effort that scrapes along on the backs of other minimally funded projects. It's one-of-a-kind work is meant to plant the seeds of accountability in this otherwise justice-barren land.

Naming the Ones We Lost is what it's called. Cofounded by Anyieth D'Awol, a South Sudanese then splitting her time between Brooklyn and Mozambique, the project aims to do just what it says since neither the government, nor the opposition, nor any foreign NGO, aid organization, or civil society group has bothered to identify the victims of South Sudan's conflict. In December 2014—the first anniversary of the outbreak of the fighting—the project released a list of names of civilians and soldiers, men and women, students and farmers, doctors and pastoralists, U.N. peacekeepers and foreigners of various nationalities killed in the war. Most, however, were South Sudanese, most were civilians, and most were young. It's just a beginning, given a grim record that would undoubtedly fill hundreds of such pages, but I flip through the 15 on hand, a spreadsheet of pain, regret, and loss, listing names, ages, and the dates and locations of death including:

Amuc Liebo Amuc, 11, March 2014, Malakal
Angelina Lokuru Longar Lochebe, 81–85, December 2013, Juba
Chal Chol Nyakwan, 15, March 2014, Owaci, Upper Nile
Josephina Ayul Atik, 12, January 2014, Malakal
Julius Taban Fredre Lodo, 28, December 2013, Bor
Monica Nakang Marco Loboi, 31–35, December 2013, Juba
Nhial Makuach Gok, 14, April 2014, Bentiu
Simon Nyang Lam, 46, n/a, Bor
Wilson Ayul Atik, 14, January 2014, Malakal
And on and on it goes…

"This list, although a fraction of the total loss, reflects the devastating human impact of South Sudan's year-long war in which no one has been officially counting the dead. Peace remains elusive, mass graves dot the landscape with civilians, both young and old, bearing the brunt of the fighting," reads a portion of the cover sheets that accompany the 572 names (later amended to 568 due to duplicates).

"We were warned not to do it because everyone was scared that people will start fighting again, which is really strange to think that people would start fighting because of a list of names of people killed in the fighting," says D'Awol, a willowy woman with striking brown eyes and a powerful presence. "It didn't happen, thankfully. But there was a very strange silence about everything we had done." For her, naming is just a first step. She's also begun work on mapping incidents of violence and trying to sort out the parties responsible. Neither is an easy task given the nature of the conflict and the difficulty of getting corroborating information in an environment webbed with fear, misinformation, ethnic tension, and government interference. "One side is claiming 20,000 or 24,000 killed in Juba and the other side, the government, is completely denying it. And the supporters of the rebels don't want to acknowledge any others were killed in such big numbers by their soldiers. That's why we have to name people—so that we can start saying, 'Where and how was this person killed?'"

Some of the names, D'Awol tells me, were gathered from news articles and human rights reports. Many more, says Yakani, come from eyewitness testimony. He shows me a binder filled with "South Sudan Eye Witness Declaration Forms," a multi-page questionnaire designed to gather data for the project by logging information about the witness—name, age, sex, ethnicity, relationship (if any) to a victim of violence—the types of incidents (e.g., murder, rape, looting, physical assault), and other relevant material, in addition to full narratives told at length. He says that they have around 10 more binders like it, about 700 individual forms, already an encyclopedia of horrors and they've barely begun. The information on each form is later logged into a database and researchers work to verify it against other sources.

Much of the information is gathered at U.N. Protection of Civilians sites. There, CEPO runs programs teaching various "life skills"—crocheting, tie-dying, making purses out of wooden beads—which allow staff to reach out to the population and distribute the questionnaires. "We use this project as the point of intervention to build up trust," he explains of the life-skills work. "They have confidence in us so they will participate in projects like Naming." There's an added reason that "Naming" piggybacks on other projects: it's completely unfunded, relying on volunteers and whatever funds can be scraped together from other CEPO efforts. Several NGOs, Yakani tells me, passed on supporting it.

While donors and the public at large have been wary, many victims and witnesses have reacted favorably to the naming efforts, he says, before offering a few caveats. For instance, when news about a possible agreement on reconciliation and power-sharing emerges from the intermittent peace talks between Kiir and Machar's negotiators in Addis Ababa, Ethiopia, without talk of justice and accountability, it directly impacts the naming project, Yakani explains. "The expectations are high in terms of the quest for justice and accountability. People say, 'You have collected the names, but when will we get justice?' So we have to engage in expectation management…"

Yakani preaches a strategy of activism and self-reliance instead of waiting for the government, the International Criminal

Court, the African Union, or some other outside body to take action and solve South Sudan's accountability problems. Instead, he calls on aggrieved South Sudanese to press for change themselves. "We try to explain that they as citizens have responsibilities and duties to push for justice and accountability," he tells me. "We take a human rights approach. Demand your rights, but you have the responsibility to hold others accountable. We explain that we are engaged in gathering evidence and facts that can empower them to take action, no matter what happens in Addis. But that's the limit. So [we tell them] they cannot give up on putting pressure on leaders for accountability."

To help facilitate such a program in South Sudan's challenging human rights environment, CEPO is now trying to educate internally displaced persons about their rights, so that they will have more confidence in exercising them. It's a major task, one of many along what will be, at best, a long road to achieving any measure of justice.

But can ordinary people, much less those displaced and in desperate circumstances, truly agitate for justice in a nation where investigations are buried, journalists are disappeared, and the National Security Service is, as one senior U.N. official told me, a law unto itself? "They're the puppet masters. There's no law controlling them. They have, by law, no right to arrest people, but they do it. It's a disruptive organization."

D'Awol, a former U.N. human rights officer and the founder and director of the ROOTS Project, a civil society organization based in Juba, tells me about the coercive surveillance she came under in late 2014.[140] "My last week in Juba, I noticed I was being followed by National Security," she recalls. "It was terrible. Four people, every day, all day. Just sitting there and watching me. It was very scary. And you wonder 'Who authorized you... who are you and who sent you?' People are already going missing. The situation is so bad. If you speak out, people just go quiet around you because either you're a rebel—and you're going to be arrested, you're part of National Security and trying to entrap people, or you're insane. So nobody says anything. It's horrible."

In 2015, as I'm finishing up my work in South Sudan, I try getting back in touch with Edmund Yakani to no avail. I call and call but can't get through. I send emails that aren't returned. I assume I've become such a pain that he's now screening my calls but decide to give him a last try one night at around 8 p.m. and, after four or five rings, he finally picks up. I can barely say hello before Yakani unleashes a torrent of apologies and explanations. Between his high-speed speech and the crackly connection, I'm only able to pick up bits and pieces. I fold open the first notebook I can get my hands on and scrawl down whatever I can catch: "death threat," "South Sudan Law Society," "National Security."

"When can we talk?" I ask. He says he can meet me early the next morning. I'm waiting at the appointed spot when he arrives around 8 a.m. to explain exactly what happened. He was at a meeting of the South Sudan Law Society, a civil society organization that promotes justice and human rights, when he received a phone call from his office. Representatives of one of CEPO's donors had just showed up and urgently needed to see him, so Yakani excused himself from the meeting and returned to the office. But the donors were no donors. They were, he quickly realized, agents from the National Security Service. They told Yakani to come with them and when he refused, they shoved him out the door and into their car. They drove him around and finally out toward the grounds of the old Ethiopian Embassy and then stopped the car. "They said 'Look, we know what you're doing… You're one of these critics of the government involved with naming and shaming.' I asked them who gave the orders. Can they show me a warrant? They said, 'It came from above.'"

After about 15 minutes, Yakani adds, they kicked him out of the car. His understated assessment: "This is how they express their frustration."

Yakani has been drawing ire for years, so why did they pick him up now? "We do issue monthly reports on media incidents," he notes, pointing out that he had been strenuously advocating for the release of journalist George Livio, held incommunicado and without charge since August 2014.[141] "I've also been tweeting about the 'last resort option' concerning the peace talks," he adds, referring to the possibility that the rest of the world could impose sanctions on South Sudan, including an arms embargo. Yakani goes on to name several other projects that sound no less likely as candidates for provoking government anger.

I express fear for his safety and he responds, "For me, it's a normal thing. It's a war."

In the wake of the incident, he tells me, "I set up mechanisms. I called for physical protection." Being an American, my mind wandered to bulletproof vests, sidearms, and burly bodyguards, but Yakani has something else entirely in mind: friends in high places—foreign friends, like U.S. ambassador Charles Twining. Having him visit the office, having his car out front or U.N. vehicles in the parking lot, or having visits by other foreign officials with clout is the way Yakani sends a message to the government to back off. It is, in fact, the only viable insurance policy he's got.

"Yesterday, three ambassadors visited the office. The U.K. ambassador was with me in the office in the morning hours. In the afternoon, it was Norway's ambassador and the U.S. ambassador in the evening. And this morning, after 9 a.m., I'm expecting the

Dutch ambassador and at midday the E.U. ambassador." They've told him that, if he needs another round of visits, he should just pick up the phone.

That's all well and good when Yakani is at work, but what about when the father of two is at home? That's a more daunting situation, he explains, as he and his family don't live in the most secure area. Their home isn't in a compound with concrete walls. All it has is a bamboo fence. If agents come for him, he'll have little time to make the calls that might save him from being disappeared. He does talk about trying to raise funds for a more secure home or to hire a security guard to offer some modicum of protection, but when you're with him you sense that this is a reassuring fantasy, not reality.

Although Yakani has some invitations to speak overseas about the human rights situation in South Sudan, he fears not being allowed back in the country. He suspects, in fact, that the government may be ratcheting up the heat to get him to leave. Some colleagues, especially in the international human rights community, he says, have urged him to do exactly that for his safety.

"Quitting is not an option," he tells me. If he leaves South Sudan now, he explains, the government would be able to cast him as a "foreign-aided voice." In addition, colleagues and emerging activists would be cowed. "As I said, for me it's a type of war. I can't give up protecting human rights. I'll never give up." Those are some of his last words to me before he jumps on the back of a boda-boda and heads for the CEPO office to meet the Dutch ambassador.

I watch him disappear in the distance, wondering if I'll see him again, wondering how long foreign ambassadors and human rights groups can keep him safe. He says that the list that Naming the Ones We Lost will unveil in December 2015 will have more than 1,000 names on it.

In a statement accompanying their first list, Yakani and D'Awol wrote: "We invite all South Sudanese citizens and friends of South Sudan to join in this remembering and continue submitting names until all those who have been lost are publicly named," When that might be is anybody's guess.

◆

The stretch of Guedele Road leading up to the turn—a swath of wide, unmarred blacktop bracketed by rutted dirt—is about as smooth as roads get in Juba, which is to say as smooth as it gets in South Sudan. This main drag, a wide boulevard with tall, completely atypical streetlights down the center, is a commercial paradise, lined with countless shops selling furniture and linoleum tiles, a storefront with a sign reading "Comrades for Catering and Services," the Gudele Furniture Mart, and most days a stand selling fruit beneath two bright pink umbrellas embossed with the logo of Zain, a local cellular service carrier, and its slogan: "A Wonderful World."

Without warning, the turn is upon me. There's no street sign, no indication of what this place might be. Had I kept on down Guedele Road, the blacktop would have quickly vanished and, just after a butcher shop and a small bridge, I'd see a large compound sitting on a small rise, its tall blue walls topped with bulbous coils of razor wire. A sign over its main gate reads: "Please Respect the Law and the Law Respects You!" It's the Central Equatoria State Police Station. But I'm not looking for a police station, I'm looking for the Police Building and so I turn right and follow the still smooth road as it dips down into a quieter, more ominous place where the law and respect for it, on the part of the state, was obliterated in December 2013.

Just beyond the turn, a knot of men sit on blue plastic chairs soaking up the shade provided by the branches of an old mango tree. They're in civilian clothes—long-sleeve, button-down shirts, pants with crisp creases. Near them, two men are standing; the taller of them, middle-aged and bald, wears a tan suit. The other, in a short-sleeved shirt, gives me a long, hard stare, his eyes narrowing as his left arm bends and his hand finds his hip. His demeanor suggests displeasure and his expression is clear. I'm not welcome.

Just beyond him, I see it clearly for the first time. It's unlike any other building I've seen in the area and its outer wall has, to my untutored eye, a Moorish look to it. This, I'm certain, is the place I've been looking for.

This is the Gudele Police Building, the site where hundreds of men were crammed into a tiny room on December 15, 2013. The site where some of them were smothered to death from the crush of bodies, the soaring temperatures, the lack of water, and others were hauled out and shot nearby. Somewhere around here, many others stood waiting, worrying, sweating until bullets began ripping through the windows, ricocheting through the room, tearing flesh, smashing bone, leaving the living covered by the dead, hundreds of dead, 386 corpses, according to Felix Taban.

More than a year later there are, of course, no bodies, no viscera, no blood. It was washed away long ago by the SPLA and Taban's men. And I can't see any obvious bullet holes anywhere. It's been like this for my entire reporting trip. Physical evidence regularly eludes me.

I ask just about everyone I can if they know the whereabouts of mass graves—secret sites where bodies may have been buried by the government or the rebels. I get a lot of vague answers. I get a lot of general locations. I take cursory looks at a couple of sites, but find nothing definitive. Some suspected locations are in off-limits, militarily protected areas—effectively no-go zones. One informant tells me he knows of six mass graves: three around

Juba, two in Malakal, and one in Bor. He says he even has GPS locations for the three sites in the capital. I ask if he'll lead me there. He tells me to call him later that day at an appointed time to arrange it. But when I call, there's no answer. I reach out for days after with no luck. He never calls me back.

◆

I take it as personal failure that I couldn't verify even one site in or around Juba where corpses were secreted away, where the sins of young armed men and the older men they serve were swallowed up by the earth. But reflecting on it later, I wonder just what I thought I would find and what it would mean. Would bones add so much more? The names, the stories, the witnesses are more important.

It's the living, who—sometimes at great personal peril—will tell the story of this conflict: Simon Wuor and Felix Taban and Ayak and Martha. It's the work of those like Anyieth D'Awol and Edmund Yakani and their colleagues and the hundreds who have given testimony, who had the courage to name names that may someday make a difference, if anything does. One day, they or others like them may be able to create monuments, memorials, sites of remembrance that will at least gesture at the horror of this war, that will force people to remember and acknowledge, if not atone.

At Auschwitz, human hair—black, brown, red, white, blond—almost two tons of it, lies piled behind glass.[142] At the killing field in Choeung Ek, Cambodia, you walk on paths laced with fragments of human bones, and in a shrine, find skulls, thousands of them.[143] At the rear of the Ntarama Church in Rwanda, skulls and other bones line a set of metal shelves. In the front, by the altar, lie weapons wielded by the killers—machetes, knives, a club, even a shot put ball used to crush the skulls of some particularly unfortunate victims.[144]

Will the bones of the men slaughtered in Guedele ever be located, disinterred, and brought back to the Police Building? Will this site one day serve as a reminder, a caution, a remembrance? Will the December 2013 massacre be the last one here or will it be just one more horror in a long line of them?

Most people I speak with in South Sudan—locals and internationals, the highly educated and the illiterate, backers of the government and those with opposition sympathies, military men and civil society activists alike—believe more violence is coming, more atrocities, more bloodshed. Afraid for his job, perhaps his life, a civil servant with an intimate knowledge of human rights abuses in the current civil war asks me not to use his name so that he can speak freely and then tells me just how truly frightened he is for his country.

If violence flares into a renewed bout of nationwide warfare, he says, it will mark the end of South Sudan. This isn't the normal response I get from people here, but he isn't the average observer either, so I ask him to explain. "The whole thing will collapse," he declares. What he adds next conjures up for me the catalogue of horrors compiled by humanity over the last century: Bergen-Belsen and My Lai and Srebrenica, Guernica, Hamburg, and Hiroshima, not to mention No Gun Ri, Sharpeville, Hue, El Mozote, Sabra and Shatila, Tiananmen Square, 9/11, Haditha; Congo and China and the Soviet Union and Cambodia; Iraq and Afghanistan and Chechnya and Syria. The record is hideous. The long, snaking trail of truth commissions attests to it: Argentina, Chile, El Salvador, Guatemala, Uganda, Chad, Haiti, Bolivia, Uruguay, Zimbabwe, Nepal, South Africa, Sri Lanka, Burundi, Ecuador, Nigeria, Sierra Leone, Ghana, South Korea, Kenya, and on and on. Will South Sudan ever set up such a commission and make this list? My interviewee doesn't think so. The war will explode anew, he believes, and when it does the dead from Guedele and Bor and Malakal and Bentiu and all the other places that no one has even attempted to count will be joined by countless others.[145]

Sometimes, South Sudanese would bring up with me the specter of the Rwandan genocide, the 1994 slaughter that saw 800,000 to 1 million men, women, and children—most of them ethnic Tutsis—murdered by Hutu militias in 100 days; about 333 deaths an hour, more than five lives taken each minute, as the great chronicler of that bloodbath, Philip Gourevitch, observed.[146] If a similar slaughter were to occur in South Sudan, it would mean somewhere in the neighborhood of 1.3 million deaths; so many corpses as to be nearly incomprehensible.

But this, it seems, is exactly what Victor Lado Caesar of the South Sudan Human Rights Commission foresees—or perhaps something even worse. I ask him, as I have almost everyone else, about impunity and the lack of justice in his country and what the international community can do about them. He pauses and the silence causes me to look up from my notepad. He sighs and frowns and shakes his head slowly. After the next round of violence, Caesar says, such talk will seem ludicrous. He tells me that something Santo Laku Pio, Auxiliary Bishop of Juba's Catholic Archdiocese, had recently said was apt and paraphrases it. Fixing me with a grave look he tells me, "No one will be talking about accountability or human rights or those things. The international community will be coming here just to count the dead."[147]

Afterword

My face was slick with sweat when I made the mistake of walking onto the earthen landing strip. The wind, already steady, suddenly whipped up, sending soil airborne, stinging my eyes, coating my forehead, turning my stubble into a full beard of dirt. Defeated by the elements, I trudged to a double-padlocked corrugated metal hut and stood in the shade wondering when—or if—a helicopter would arrive and whether there would be a place for me on board.

I hung my rucksack from one of the roughhewn tree limbs holding up a metal awning that stretched out from the crudely built zinc shack. It wasn't long before a couple of young, completely naked boys came calling. They hoped I would give them something, but I had little of use to a child. Instead, I offered a weak smile and they graciously took it.

One of the tiny boys wandered away while the other began poking at the crimson compression sack holding a tent that was lashed to my backpack. Before long, an older boy—perhaps eight or nine—walked up, shooed away the youngster and nodded at me, his chin leading the way. He wore a filthy, faded purple shirt, canary yellow shorts, and had an oversized blue flip-flop on his left foot. In one hand, he carried a tattered piece of blue and white plastic that had almost certainly been a bag in a previous life, in the other, a tiny scrap of cardboard. He very deliberately laid the latter on the ground and sat on it, spreading his pencil-thin legs wide. Almost immediately, he began sifting through the dirt and rocks, every so often picking up something tiny and carefully placing it on the plastic. He did this methodically and meticulously. From several feet away, looking over his shoulder, I could just make out the prizes he was finding. Apparently, a bag of dried red beans had sprung a leak and spilled some of its contents there. With patience, the legumes could be recovered, one bean at a time, from the dirt and rocks.

It didn't take me long to begin feeling like a heel standing there, waiting for a helicopter to whisk me back to the capital and my hotel whose restaurant serves oversized hamburgers and cold beer. In a few more days, I'd be back in the United States with its far more lavish creature comforts. I shook my head, thrust out my bottom lip and exhaled, using my breath to cool my dirt-streaked face as I contemplated this boy—and me. Then I hoisted my bag onto my back, adjusted its straps, and walked out into the blazing sun and away from his work space.

That boy was far from the most desperate child I had seen in South Sudan, but he stuck in my mind—the care he took in spreading out the torn bag, the disciplined way he sifted through the dirt, his workman-like demeanor. He had probably recovered about 30 tiny, crimson beans by the time I left. He deserved so much better.

And he wasn't—he isn't—alone.

◆

"America's obligation to South Sudan," read the headline on the July 29, 2015, *New York Times* editorial the day I first sat down to write this afterword. "The country, after all, is America's foster child," noted the piece, pointing to the major roles played by the administrations of George W. Bush and Barack Obama in its independence. "Today, South Sudan is among the most tragic stories in Africa, caught in a brutal and ever-growing power struggle … that has left thousands dead, millions displaced, and half the population in danger of starvation."[1]

Indeed, the situation was awful while I was reporting there in 2014 and worse when I returned in 2015. It continued to go downhill thereafter. I wrapped up my reporting in Jonglei in March 2015. The next month, the SPLA and rebel forces clashed in the northern part of the state.[2] Not long after, the Protection of Civilians site in Juba from which I had reported over the course of several weeks was rocked by battles between two Nuer groups, leaving one dead and dozens injured.[3]

The situation was far worse in Unity State. The U.N. base near its capital, Bentiu, experienced another flood of displaced people. They arrived with stories of increasingly brutal behavior by government troops and allied militia. "I was with my neighbor when they asked whether her baby was a boy or a girl," a woman who escaped to that sanctuary from the town of Koch told a Human Rights Watch interviewer. "When she said 'boy' they told her that they were going to kill the baby because 'when he grows up he will fight with us so I have to kill him before that happens.' They shot the boy in front of his mother."

This was just one of the many horrors chronicled by the United Nations and Human Rights Watch. Another woman from Koch County told of being dragged from her home by government soldiers and gang-raped alongside her neighbor, while her three-year-old child looked on.[4]

"Watch how we will rape your daughter," government-allied militiamen told still another woman from the same area before they assaulted her younger daughter right in front of her. Then they turned to her other daughter and did the same. "When they finished with her, they burned our tukul" the mother told a Human Rights Watch researcher. "They then grabbed her and held her down in a fire and burned her face, her shoulder, and the length of her body." When she caught fire, they finally let her go. She was too badly injured to run, so her mother and younger sister left her in the bush when they fled.[5]

A witness from Mayendit saw SPLA troops castrate a man and a teenage boy.[6] A woman from Rubchier village recounted the killing of four people by government armored vehicles. "They were running with the tanks after the people and then after they hit them they would roll back over them to confirm they were dead," she recalled.[7]

"Horrible things are happening and people just ignore it," Anyieth D'Awol, one of the founders of the Naming the Ones We Lost project, tells me as we sit in a kosher French bistro in Park Slope, Brooklyn, two months after I return to the United States. "Somehow, there has got to be some accountability." She's right, of course, and yet her wish couldn't sound more like a pipedream. Who, I wonder, is going to hold war criminals to account as South Sudan slides deeper into violence? And what will the people I interviewed, the people I spent time with, the people who generously spoke with a stranger about their upended lives, do in the weeks and months ahead?

In a world awash in chaos and war, with refugees fleeing both, at a time when men, women, and children are dying in desperate attempts to reach sanctuary in Europe from conflicts in Afghanistan and Iraq and Libya and Syria, what's to become of the people of South Sudan: Martha and Ayak; Nyanachiek and her children; the men and women marooned on U.N. bases; the child veterans from Pibor; the roughly 2.5 million people displaced inside or outside the country?

◆

Beginning in the 1980s, the efforts of an eclectic, bipartisan coalition of American supporters—Washington activists, evangelical Christians, influential congressional representatives, celebrities, a presidential administration focused on regime change and nation-building, and another that picked up the mantle—helped "midwife" South Sudan into existence.[8]

Perhaps no country in Africa received as much congressional attention. And on July 9, 2011, its Independence Day, President Barack Obama released a stirring statement. "I am confident that the bonds of friendship between South Sudan and the United States will only deepen in the years to come. As Southern Sudanese undertake the hard work of building their new country, the United States pledges our partnership as they seek the security, development, and responsive governance that can fulfill their aspirations and respect their human rights." In August 2012, Secretary of State Hillary Clinton, speaking in Juba, was emphatic that the U.S. "commitment to this new nation is enduring and absolute in terms of assistance and aid and support going forward."[9]

What are the ongoing obligations of a midwife? How solid are the bonds of friendship between the United States and South Sudan? How solemn was Obama's pledge of partnership and Clinton's of enduring support?

For years, the United States has dumped untold billions of dollars into regime-change operations, nation-building schemes, military interventions, and interminable wars in the Greater Middle East. Iraqis and Afghans, Syrians, Libyans, and Yemenis have grappled with the consequences. South Sudan was a different type of American intervention, but the results turned out to be sadly similar for its people.

The United States provided some roads and electricity, built up the army, and poured a great deal of money into the new nation. Now, it's reduced to providing humanitarian aid as part of an international effort to fend off the famine that's forever knocking on the young country's door. For all I know, the red beans that boy was picking out of the dirt were "from the American people"—as big bags of U.S. Agency for International Development sorghum, rice, lentils, and other emergency staples are branded the world over.

But is that enough?

Is it enough for a man to feel ashamed and leave a, rail-thin child to pluck spilled beans from the dirt? Is it enough for a country to pledge enduring commitment and instead provide just enough food aid to keep the nation it fostered on life support? This is not to say that the United States has offered a trivial sum.[10] The approximately $1.3 billion spent on relief efforts since the country plunged in civil war in 2013 is significant.[11] At least until you realize that a year of ineffective efforts bombing the Islamic State in Iraq and Syria cost about three times that amount.[12]

"The United States will support the people of South Sudan as they begin the implementation process, but it is imperative that the parties remain committed to peace," National Security Advisor Susan Rice announced on August 26, 2015, after a peace deal was signed between Salva Kiir and Riek Machar. "Together, we must help South Sudan implement the agreement, to stave off famine, to stand steadfast and united against those who block the path to peace, and to hold accountable those who have committed atrocities."[13]

Since the civil war began, American officials have made a series of similar statements to little effect. Whether this peace deal holds or crumbles like the many cease fires before it, the United States faces a choice: Will it lavish the sort of taxpayer dollars it normally devotes to war-making on its foster child or will it leave this fledgling, fractured country with beans, platitudes, and little else?

"The United States will continue to support the aspirations of all Sudanese," declared President Obama at the close of his statement on South Sudan's Independence Day in 2011. "Together, we can ensure that today marks another step forward in Africa's long journey toward opportunity, democracy, and justice."[14] In nation-building projects from Afghanistan to Iraq, military interventions from Libya to Yemen, military aid efforts from Mali to Burkina Faso, the United States has turned out to be remarkably inept when it comes to providing opportunities, the basics for democratic polities, or justice of any imaginable kind. Invariably, such normally military-oriented or -led American endeavors have ended in failure, disappointment, and in a number of cases outright fiasco.

As South Sudan was midwifed into nationhood "by any means necessary," atrocities from the 1990s and earlier were swept under the rug, only to have them resurface in recent years. Will history repeat itself? Will the United States and its international partners make every conceivable effort "to hold accountable those who have committed atrocities" in order to help achieve a permanent peace? Or will they take an easier road—one that silences the guns of today only to have them ring out anew with even greater fury at the dawn of some distant tomorrow—or perhaps even sooner? It remains to be seen whether the United States will "stand steadfast," step back, or walk away from the nation it spent so much time and effort ushering into existence—and whether it matters at all what course South Sudan's foster parent charts.

Acknowledgments

My reporting for this book would have been impossible without the generous support of Lannan Foundation. My heartfelt thanks go out to Patrick Lannan and Sarah Knopp for recognizing the importance of listening to the voices of South Sudanese and allowing me the privilege of hearing them firsthand. The foundation has come through for me too many times to count and I owe the women and men there, who do so much good work, an immense debt of gratitude.

The foundations of my 2015 reporting in South Sudan were laid during my 2014 trip which was made possible by Esther Kaplan, Joe Conason, and Sarah Blaustain of the Nation Institute's Investigative Fund as well as by the generosity of Adelaide Gomer. They all have my enduring thanks.

I'm eternally grateful to Taya Kitman and her staff at The Nation Institute who have provided me with an intellectual home for so many years.

This book would, of course, not exist without all the South Sudanese whose voices appear in the preceding pages (and many who do not)—women, men, and children who gave so freely of themselves and taught me so much. I'm grateful for their trust and time. I especially want to thank Anyieth D'Awol and Edmund Yakani.

I also owe a great debt to the expert work of a number of fine drivers, fixers, and translators, especially Ruot George who, I hope, will one day be able to report again from a peaceful South Sudan.

Skye Wheeler and Jehanne Henry of Human Rights Watch lent assistance in innumerable ways while I was reporting. Jehanne read an early draft of the book—no small task—and offered sage advice and spot-on critiques. Skye read a later version and provided equally smart comments and suggestions. I can't thank them enough for this, nor their important work on South Sudan that informed so much of my reporting.

Roane Carey of the *Nation* was instrumental in facilitating the reporting in this book. I'm also grateful for the ample assistance provided by Dijana Kondres, Aziz Haidari, Chandrasekhar Pakala, Shantal Persaud, Ariane Quentier, and Joe Contreras of the U.N. Mission in South Sudan. Claire McKeever, Kate Donovan, and Doune Porter of UNICEF were all instrumental in getting me to Pibor and have my thanks, as does the U.N. Humanitarian Air Service which flew me there.

A well-placed source with the U.N. offered me candid opinions and assistance when I needed it. Aid workers with a number of NGOs including Oxfam, Médecins Sans Frontières, the International Rescue Committee, and Nonviolent Peaceforce, provided advice and information and have my sincere gratitude.

Many thanks as well to Anthony Arnove, Nisha Bolsey, Rachel Cohen, Julie Fain, Rory Fanning, Jason Farbman, Eric Kerl, Jon Kurinsky, John McDonald, Jim Plank, Behzad Ragian, Jesus Ramos, Bill Roberts, Ahmed Shawki, and Dao X. Tran at Haymarket Books, along with Brian Baughan who proofread the book, for all of their time and efforts.

My editor and friend Tom Engelhardt was the first to suggest the raw manuscript that emerged from this reporting trip could, indeed, be a book. Then he put in the editing elbow grease to see that it was.

Dana Blaney did me huge favors during my reporting—and it wasn't the first time. Thanks for having my back, cuz!

Most of all, I want to thank Tam for putting up with the absences and the worry and for making it all possible. Your smile lights my way, your voice lifts me up, you're my Polaris guiding me home—my always and everything.

Notes

A More Personal War

1. Central Intelligence Agency, "South Sudan" in The World Factbook, https://www.cia.gov/library/publications/the-world-factbook /geos/od.html; Louisa Lombard, "A Page from Khartoum's Play-book," *New York Times* (February 20, 2012), http://latitude.blogs .nytimes.com/2012/02/20/south-sudan-like-khartoum-oppresses -ethnic-minority/?_r=0.
2. "South Sudan President Salva Kiir Signs Peace Deal," BBC.com (August 26, 2015), http://www.bbc.com/news/world-africa -34066511.

Next Time They'll Come to Count the Dead

1. Edmund Yakani, 2/9/15 interview.
2. Human Rights Watch, *South Sudan's New War: Abuses by Government and Opposition Forces* (August 2014), 2.
3. United Nations Mission in South Sudan (UNMISS), *Conflict in South Sudan: A Human Rights Report* (May 8, 2014), 16; Human Rights Watch, *South Sudan's New War*, 23.
4. Simon Wuor, 2/13/15 interview.
5. UNMISS, *Conflict in South Sudan*, 18–19; Human Rights Watch,

South Sudan's New War, 27.

6. Human Rights Watch, *South Sudan's New War*, 31.

7. Wuor's cousins survived. Simon Wuor, 2/13/15 interview.

8. Human Rights Watch, *South Sudan's New War*, 31; Skye Wheeler, email message to Nick Turse (February 14, 2015).

9. Thudan, 2/18/15 interview.

10. Human Rights Watch, *South Sudan's New War*, 31; Skye Wheeler, electronic mail message to Nick Turse (February 14, 2015).

11. Gatthuoy Gatkoi, 2/24/15 interview.

12. Human Rights Watch, *South Sudan's New War*, 24.

13. UNMISS, *Conflict in South Sudan*, 17–19; Human Rights Watch, *South Sudan's New War*, 26.

14. Sheldon Wardwell, email to Dave (December 16, 2013).

15. Wardwell, 2/19/15 interview.

16. "Two South Sudan Aid Workers Killed," Radio Tamazuj (December 23, 2013), https://radiotamazuj.org/en/article/two-south -sudan-aid-workers-killed.

17. South Sudan Human Rights Commission, *Interim Report on South Sudan Internal Conflict, December 15, 2013–March 15, 2014*, 11.

18. Mak Banguot Gok, "Dr. Riek Machar Is Sanctified of Not Signing Ostentatious Proposal in Expense of Over 20,000 Nuer Acquitted Lives Lost in Juba," SouthSudan.net, http://www.southsudan.net /drriek.html.

19. Ibrahim Wani, 2/17/15 interview.

20. Victor Lado Caeser, 3/4/15 interview.

21. Human Rights Watch, *South Sudan's New War*, 27; UNMISS, *Conflict in South Sudan*, 59; South Sudan Human Rights Commission, *Interim Report on South Sudan Internal Conflict*, 11.

22. Ibrahim Wani, 2/17/15 interview.

23. Senior United Nations official, interview.

24. Roda Nyajiech Juch, 2/9/15 interview.

25. Senior United Nations official, interview.

26. Name withheld, 2/13/15 interview.

27. UNMISS, *Conflict in South Sudan*, 3, 22; Human Rights Watch,

South Sudan's New War, 36–37.

28. Human Rights Watch, *South Sudan's New War*, 37.

29. Daniel Howden, "South Sudan: The State That Fell Apart in a Week," *Guardian* (December 23, 2013), http://www.theguardian.com/world/2013/dec/23/south-sudan-state-that-fell-apart-in-a-week.

30. Somini Sengupta, "A Top U.N. Rights Official Describes 'Horror' in South Sudan," *New York Times* (January 17, 2014), http://www.nytimes.com/2014/01/18/world/africa/south-sudan.html?_r=0.

31. UNMISS, *Conflict in South Sudan*, 3.

32. Human Rights Watch, *South Sudan's New War*, 22.

33. Mangok had been in command of the forces that fought rebel Nuer troops around the General Headquarters on December 16. Human Rights Watch, *South Sudan's New War*, 29.

34. "Kiir's Guard Commander and Rebel General First on US Sanctions List," Radio Tamazuj (May 6, 2015), https:// radiotamazuj.org/en/article/kiir%E2%80%99s-guard-commander-and-rebel-general-first-names-us-sanctions-list.

35. A Dinka resident of the area reported seeing troops move "huge" numbers of bodies into the trucks. Human Rights Watch, *South Sudan's New War*, 38; Taban, 2/13/15 interview; Taban 2/24/15 interview.

36. Jehanne Henry, "Dispatches: Is the Truth Off-Limits in Juba, South Sudan?" Human Rights Watch (February 18, 2014), http://www.hrw.org/news/2014/02/18/dispatches-truth-limits-juba-south-sudan.

37. Sheldon Wardwell, 2/19/15 interview.

38. Rudolf Carl Slatin, *Fire and Sword in the Sudan: A Personal Narrative of Fighting and Serving the Dervishes* (New York: Edward Arnold, 1896).

39. Deborah Scroggins, *Emma's War: An Aid Worker, a Warlord, Radical Islam, and the Politics of Oil—a True Story of Love and Death in Sudan* (New York: Pantheon, 2002).

40. International Crisis Group, "South Sudan: Jonglei—We Have

Always Been at War," *Africa Report*, no. 221 (December 22, 2014), http://www.crisisgroup.org/~/media/Files/africa/horn -of-africa/south%20sudan/221-south-sudan-jonglei-we-have -always-been-at-war.pdf; Stephanie Beswick, *Sudan's Blood Memory: The Legacy of War, Ethnicity, and Slavery in Early South Sudan* (Rochester, NY: University of Rochester Press, 2004).

41. "Sudan – First Civil War," GlobalSecurity.org, http://www .globalsecurity.org/military/world/war/sudan-civil-war1.htm.

42. Frontline, "Sudan: Facts and Stats," http://www.pbs.org /frontlineworld/stories/sudan/facts.html.

43. Scroggins, *Emma's War*; Mike Woolridge, "Lasting Legacy of Ethiopia's Famine," BBC.com (October 23, 2009), http://news .bbc.co.uk/2/hi/africa/8321043.stm.

44. Scroggins, *Emma's War*.

45. For examples, see Eric Marsden, "'Skeletons' Flee from Famine and Mass Slaughter." *Sunday Times* (London, England) (May 1, 1988), 22.

46. Associated Press, "Sudan Reports Rebels Killed 83 in Massacre," *New York Times* (January 15, 1986).

47. Riek Machar Teny-Dhurgon, "South Sudan: A History of Political Domination" (Philadelphia: University of Pennsylvania, African Studies Center, 1995), http://www.africa.upenn.edu /Hornet/sd._machar.html; Jane Perlez, "Of Sudan's Woes, War Is the Worst," *New York Times* (October 19, 1988); Eric Marsden,"Refugees Killed in Sudan Massacre," *Sunday Times* (May 17, 1987), 16.

48. Jemera Rone, John Prendergast, and Karen Sorensen, *Civilian Devastation: Abuses by All Parties in the War in Southern Sudan*, Human Rights Watch (January 1, 1994), 135; Judith McCallum, "Murle Identity in Post-Colonial South Sudan" (unpublished PhD dissertation, York University, Toronto), referenced in Edward Thomas, *South Sudan: A Slow Liberation* (London: Zed Books, 2015).

49. UNMISS, *Conflict in South Su- dan*, 14–15; Human Rights Watch, "South Sudan: Ethnic Targeting, Widespread Killings,"

January 16, 2014, http://www.hrw.org/news/2014/01/16/south
-sudan-ethnic-targeting-widespread-killings; Jane Standley,
"Reclaiming the Past in Southern Sudan," July 1, 2006, BBC
News, http://news.bbc.co.uk/1/hi/programmes/from_our_own
_correspondent/5133324.stm.

50. Rory Nugent, "Feeding Centre Destroyed in Sudan Massacre,"
Observer (May 16, 1993).

51. Scroggins, *Emma's War*.

52. Pamela Dockins, "What Triggered the Kiir-Machar Rift in South
Sudan?" Voice of America (January 9, 2014), http://www
.voanews.com/content/what-triggered-the-kir-machar-rift-in
-south-sudan/1826903.html.

53. John Kerry, "Chairman Kerry Statement at Hearing on Sudan,"
U.S. Senate Committee on Foreign Relations (March 15, 2012),
http://www.foreign.senate.gov/press/chair/release/chairman
-kerry-statement-at-hearing-on-sudan-.

54. Rebecca Hamilton, "Special Report: The Wonks Who Sold
Washington on South Sudan," Reuters (July 11, 2012), http://
mobile.reuters.com/article/idUSBRE86A0GC20120711?irpc=932;
Federation of Ameri- can Scientists, "Sudan People's Liberation
Army (SPLA)/Sudan People's Liberation Movement (SPLM),"
http://fas.org/irp/world/para/spla.htm.

55. Donald K. Steinberg, "Remarks by USAID Deputy Administra-
tor Donald K. Steinberg to the Congressional Black Caucus
Founda tion," USAID.gov (September 23, 2011), http://www
.usaid.gov/news-information/speeches/remarks-usaid-deputy
-administrator-donald-k-steinberg-congressional-black; "U.S. Is
Facing Hard Choices in South Sudan," *New York Times* (January
3, 2014), http://www.nytimes.com/2014/01/04/us/politics
/us-is-facing-hard-choices-in-south-sudan.html?_r=0; U.S.
State Department, Bureau of African Affairs, "South Sudan –
U.S. Relations with South Sudan," Fact Sheet (September 16,
2015), www.state.gov/r/pa/ei/ bgn/171718.htm; Lauren Ploch
Blanchard, "The Crisis in South Sudan," Congressional Research
Service (January 9, 2014), http://www. google.com/url?sa=t&rct

=j&q=&esrc=s&source=web&cd=1&cad=rja&uact=8&ved
=0CCAQFjAA&url=http%3A%2F%2Fwww.fas.org%2Fsgp
%2Fcrs%2Frow%2FR43344.pdf&ei=EICQU4a2CrLQsQT5
_YDoDw&usg=AFQjCNGSn8hE0YiE1- bkK9SRBycrxWGFYA
&bvm=bv.68235269,d.cWc; Patrick McGroarty, "South Sudan's
Kiir Says Uganda Helping to Fight Rebels," *Wall Street Journal*
(January 16, 2014), http://online.wsj.com/news/articles
/SB10001424052702303465004579324240269459308.

56. "Statement of President Barack Obama Recognition of the Republic of South Sudan" (July 11, 2011), http://www.whitehouse
.gov/the-press-office/2011/07/09/statement-president-barack
-obama-recognition-republic-south-sudan.

57. Patricia Taft, "Statehood or Bust: The Case of South Sudan,"
Fund for Peace (June 24, 2014), http://library.fundforpeace.org
/fsi14-southsudan.

58. Ibid.

59. Edward Thomas, *South Sudan: A Slow Liberation* (London: Zed
Books, 2015); "South Sudan VP Confirms Apology for Bor Massacre," *Sudan Tribune* (April 3, 2012), http:// www.sudantribune
.com/spip.php?article42124.

60. "Kiir's Guard Commander and Rebel General First Names on US
Sanctions List," Radio Tamazuj.

61. Brendan Tuttle, "Life Is Prickly: Belonging and the Common
Place in Bor, Southern Sudan" (PhD dissertation, Temple University, 2013), xviii.

62. Martha, 2/15/15 interview; Ayak, 2/15/15 interview; Nyanachiek,
2/15/15 interview.

63. Martha, Ayak, Nyanachiek, 2/15/15 interviews.

64. UNMISS, *Conflict in South Sudan*, 26.

65. Ibid., 26.

66. UNMISS, *Conflict in South Sudan*, 27; Human Rights Watch,
South Sudan's New War, 49.

67. UNMISS, *Conflict in South Sudan*, 3, 29.

68. Ibid., 28.

69. Martha, Ayak, Nyanachiek, 2/15/15 interviews.

70. Skye Wheeler, 2/12/15 interview.
71. Jessica Hatcher, "Try Not to Look Away from These Terrible Killings in South Sudan," *War Is Boring* (February 10, 2014), https://medium.com/war-is-boring/try-not-to-look-away-from-these-terrible-killings-in-south-sudan-81f03448cfdd; Human Rights Watch, *South Sudan's New War*, 52.
72. Médecins Sans Frontières, "South Sudan Conflict: Violence Against Healthcare" (June 17, 2014), 14.
73. Human Rights Watch, *South Sudan's New War*, 53.
74. The Basque government claimed 1,654 civilian deaths. Later investigations put the number at around 200 to 300 killed. Jörg Diehl, "Hitler's Destruction of Guernica: Practicing Blitzkrieg in Basque Country," Spiegel Online International (April 26, 2007), http://www.spiegel.de/international/europe/hitler-s-destruction-of-guernica-practicing-blitzkrieg-in-basque-coutry-a-479675.html.
75. UNMISS, *Conflict in South Sudan*, 28.
76. Ibid., 28.
77. Ruot, 2/18/15 interview.
78. Martha, Ayak, Nyanachiek, 2/15/15 interviews.
79. UNMISS, *Conflict in South Sudan*, 26.
80. Ibid., 26–27.
81. Scroggins, *Emma's War*.
82. Nhial Majak Nhial, 2/27/15 interview.
83. Eric G. Berman and Mihaela Racovita, *Under Attack and Above Scrutiny? Arms and Ammunition Diversion from Peacekeepers in Sudan and South Sudan, 2002–14* (Geneva: Small Arms Survey/Graduate Institute of International and Development Studies, 2015), http://hsba.smallarmssurvey.org/fileadmin/docs/working-papers/HSBA-WP37-Peacekeeper-Diversions.pdf.
84. Kueth Gatkuoth, 2/24/15 interview.
85. John Kerry, "Press Availability in South Sudan," Department of State (May 2, 2014), https://geneva.usmission.gov/2014/05/03/secretary-of-state-kerry-transcript-of-press-availability-in-south-sudan/; John Kerry, "Remarks with South Sudanese

President Salva Kiir Before Their Meeting," Department of State (August 5, 2014), http://www.state.gov/secretary/remarks /2014/08/230298.htm.

86. John Kerry, "Interview with Nichola Mandil of Eye Radio," Department of State (May 4, 2015), http://www.state.gov/secretary /remarks/2015/05/241836.htm.

87. Kueth Gatkuoth, 2/24/15 interview.

88. Darlene Superville, "Obama Welcomes African Leaders for Unusual Dinner," Associated Press (August 6, 2014), http://bigstory.ap .org/article/obama-hosts-white-house-dinner-african-leaders.

89. Barack Obama, "Toast Remarks by the President at U.S.-African Leaders Summit Dinner," WhiteHouse.gov (August 5, 2014), http://www.whitehouse.gov/the-press-office/2014/08/05/toast -remarks-president-us-african-leaders-summit-dinner.

90. Barack Obama, "Remarks by President Obama to the People of Africa," WhiteHouse.gov (July 28, 2015), https://www.whitehouse .gov/the-press-office/2015/07/28/remarks-president-obama -people-africa.

91. Katy Migiro, "Uprooted South Sudanese Fear the Call to Return Home," Reuters (February 13, 2015), http://www.reuters.com /article/2015/02/13/us-southsudan-displaced-idUSKBN0LH-1HZ20150213.

92. Ibid.

93. Hoth Gor Luak, 3/4/15 interview.

94. "Juba Admits New Rebel Group Captured Mundri Town on Friday," *Sudan Tribune* (May 24, 2015), http://sudantribune.com /spip.php?article55102.

95. "David Yau Yau's Rebellion," *Human Security Baseline Assess- ment (HSBA) for Sudan and South Sudan*, Small Arms Survey, http:// www.smallarmssurveysudan.org/fileadmin/docs/facts-figures /south-sudan/armed-groups/southern-dissident-militias/HSBA -Armed-Groups-Yau-Yau.pdf.

96. Ibid.

97. John Tanza, "South Sudan Signs Peace Deal with Yau Yau Rebels," Voice of America (May 9, 2014), http://www.voanews.com

/content/south-sudan-government-signs-peace-deal-with-yau
-yau-rebels/1911603.html.

98. "South Sudanese Government, Yau Yau Rebels Sign Peace Deal,"
    Sudan Tribune (May 9, 2014), http://www.sudantribune.com
    /spip.php?article50935.

99. UNICEF, "Thousands of Children to Be Gradually Released
    from Armed Group in South Sudan," UNICEF.org (January 27,
    2015), http://www.unicef.org/southsudan/media_16067.html.

100. Ibid.

101. UNICEF, "282 Boys and 1 Girl Freed in Final Release of Children
    from Cobra Faction in South Sudan," UNICEF.org (April 24,
    2015), http://www.unicef.org/media/media_81684.html.

102. UNICEF, "Thousands of Children to Be Gradually Released."

103. Jason Patinkin, "Devastation in South Sudan Approaches Razor's
    Edge of Hunger Crisis," *Vice News* (May 28, 2015), https://news
    .vice.com/article/devastation-in-south-sudan-approaches-razors
    -edge-of-hunger-crisis; UNICEF, "South Sudan on the Edge of
    Nutrition Catastrophe if Hostilities Don't End Now," UNICEF
    .org (February 4, 2015), http://www.unicef.org/media/media
    79711.html; U.N. Office for the Coordination of Humanitarian
    Affairs, http://www.unocha.org/south-sudan/; Italian Ministry of
    Foreign Affairs and Internation- al Cooperation, "South Sudan:
    Number of Homeless People in the UN Base Rose to 119,000,"
    http://www.cooperazioneallosviluppo.esteri.it/pdgcs/index.php
    ?option=com_content&view=article&id=12321:08-05-2015
    -south-sudan-tnumber-of-homeless-people-in-the-un-base
    -rose-to-119-000&catid=117&Itemid=913.

104. Nick Turse, "The Kids Aren't All Right: Presidential Waivers,
    Child Soldiers, and an American-Made Army in Africa,"
    TomDispatch.com (May 17, 2015), http://t.co/4s0aKUNhY0.

105. Ibid.

106. Nick Turse, "As a Man-Made Famine Looms, Christmas Comes
    Early to South Sudan," TomDispatch.com (August 7, 2014),
    http://www.tomdispatch.com/blog/175878/tomgram%3A_nick
    _turse%2C_christmas_in_july_and_the_collapse_of_america

%27s_great_african_experiment; Nick Turse, "China, America, and a New Cold War in Africa? Is the Conflict in South Sudan the Opening Salvo in the Battle for a Continent?" TomDispatch. com (July 31, 2014), http://www.tomdispatch.com/post/175875 /tomgram%3A_nick_turse,_an_east-west_showdown_in_the _heart_of_africa/.

107. Turse, "The Kids Aren't All Right."

108. United Nations Security Council,"South Sudan Briefing and Consultations," *What's In Blue?* (Feb- ruary 23, 2015), http:// www.whatsinblue.org/2015/02/south-sudan-briefing-and -consultations-1.php#read-more.

109. John Tanza, "South Sudan Official Defends Delay of Human Rights Report," Voice of America (February 06, 2015), http:// www.voanews.com/content/south-sudan-human-rights-report -delay-michael-makuei/2632208.html.

110. Edmund Yakani, 2/9/15 interview.

111. Senior United Nations official, interview.

112. "South Sudan Govt Human Rights Investigation 'Ended'Report Filed with President," Radio Tamazuj (February 7, 2015), https:// radiotamazuj.org/en/article/south-sudan-government-human -rights-investigation-ended-report-filed-president; Human Rights Watch, *South Sudan's New War*.

113. Mignon T. Cardentey email to Nick Turse (March 31, 2015); Ariane Quentier email to Nick Turse (April 17, 2015).

114. Mignon T. Cardentey email to Nick Turse (March 31, 2015).

115. Henry Oyay Nyago, 2/25/15 interview.

116. Human Rights Watch, *South Sudan's New War*, 57, 59.

117. UNMISS, *Conflict in South Sudan*, 45; Human Rights Watch, *South Sudan's New War*, 60.

118. Human Rights Watch, *South Sudan's New War*, 60.

119. UNMISS, *Conflict in South Sudan*, 45.

120. Calista Burpee (formerly Pearce), 9/14/15 interview.

121. UNMISS, "Attacks on Civilians in Bentiu and Bor, April 2014" (January 9, 2015), 8.

122. Médecins Sans Frontières, "South Sudan Conflict: Violence

Against Healthcare."

123. UNMISS, "Attacks on Civilians in Bentiu and Bor, April 2014,"
8–14.

124. Human Rights Watch, *South Sudan's New War*, 69–70.

125. Ibid., 71.

126. Médecins Sans Frontières, "South Sudan Conflict: Violence
Against Healthcare."

127. Human Rights Watch, *South Sudan's New War*, 74.

128. Médecins Sans Frontières, "South Sudan Conflict: Violence
Against Healthcare."

129. Ibid.

130. UNMISS, *Conflict in South Sudan*, 37.

131. Elena Balatti, "Malakal: An Eye-Witness Diary," Gurtong.net
(March 7, 2014), http://www.gurtong.net/ECM/Editorial/tabid
/124/ctl/ArticleView/mid/519/articleId/15024/Malakal-An-Eye
-Witness-Diary.aspx; "Comboni Missionaries: About Us," http://
www.combonisouthsudan.org/index.php/who-we-are.

132. UNMISS, *Conflict in South Sudan*, 35.

133. Veronica Ayang, 2/23/15 interview.

134. UNMISS, *Conflict in South Sudan*, 35.

135. Human Rights Watch, *South Sudan's New War*, 70.

136. UNMISS, *Conflict in South Sudan*, 35.

137. "South Sudan: Preliminary UN Probe Shows Helicopter Was
Shot Down," United Nations News Centre (September 9, 2014),
http://www.un.org/apps/news/story.asp?NewsID=48674#
.VQwHZy7D7ag.

138. Associated Press, "British Aid Worker Killed in South Sudan
Capital," *New York Times* (February 18, 2015), http://abcnews.go
.com/International/wireStory/british-aid-worker-killed-south
- sudan-capital-29049846; Aislinn Laing, "British Aid Worker
Shot Dead in South Sudan Possible Victim of 'Mistaken Identity,'" *Telegraph* (February 18, 2015), http://www.telegraph.co.uk
/news/worldnews/africaandindianocean/south-sudan/11420064
/British-aid-worker-shot-dead-in-South-Sudan.html.

139. Ludovica Iaccino, "South Sudan: Journalists 'Killed by Govern-

ment Forces' to Suppress Debate on End of Civil War," *International Business Times* (February 12, 2015), http://www.ibtimes
.co.uk/south-sudan-journalists-killed-by-government-forces
-suppress-debate-end-civil-war-1487670.

140. Larisa Epatko, "At Its Third Anniversary, South Sudan Works to
Show New Brighter Side," PBS NewsHour (July 8, 2014), http://
www.pbs.org/newshour/updates/third-anniversary-south-sudan
-works-show-new-side/; Anyieth D'Awol, "IGAD Mediators, the
South Sudanese People Have the Right to Know," African Arguments (February 16, 2015), http://africanarguments.org/2015
/02/16/igad-mediators-the-south-sudanese-people-have-the
-right-to-know-by-anyieth-dawol/.

141. Peter Lokale Nakimangole, "Civil Society Demands Legal Aid
Access to UNMISS Detained Journalist," Gurtong.net (January
14, 2015), http://www.gurtong.net/ECM/Editorial/tabid/124/ctl
/ArticleView/mid/519/articleId/16039/categoryId/1/Civil-Society
-Demands-Legal-Aid-Access-To-UNMISS-Detained-Journalist
.aspx.

142. Andrew Curry, "Can Auschwitz Be Saved?" *Smithsonian Magazine* (February 2010), http://www.smithsonianmag.com/history
/can-auschwitz-be-saved-4650863/?no-ist.

143. Zoltan Istvan, "'Killing Fields' Lure Tourists in Cambodia," National Geographic Today (January 10, 2003), http://news
.nationalgeographic.com/news/2003/01/0110_030110
_tvcambodia.html;

144. "Killing Fields of Choeung Ek," LonleyPlanet.com, http://www
.lonelyplanet.com/cambodia/phnom-penh/sights/museums
-galleries/killing-fields-choeung-ek.

145. Peter Gwin, "Revisiting the Rwandan Genocide: How Churches
Became Death Traps," *National Geographic* (April 2, 2014),
http://proof.nationalgeographic.com/2014/04/02/revisiting-the
-rwandan-genocide-how-churches-became-death-traps/.

146. Civil servant, interview.

147. Philip Gourevitch, *We Wish to Inform You That Tomorrow We
Will Be Killed with Our Families: Stories from Rwanda* (New York:

Farrar, Straus and Giroux, 1998).Victor Lado Caesar, interview.

Afterword

1. "America's Obligation to South Sudan," *New York Times* (July 29, 2015), http://www.nytimes.com/2015/07/29/opinion/americas -obligation-to-south-sudan.html?_r=0.

2. United Nations Mission in the Republic of South Sudan, "Flash Human Rights Report on the Escalation of Fighting in Greater Upper Nile" (April/May 2015), http://unmiss .unmissions.org/Portals/unmiss/Reports/Final%20version %20Flash%20 Human%20Rights%20Report%20on%20the %20Escalation%20%20of%20Fighting%20in%20Greater %20Upper%20Nile.pdf.

3. "Corrected: Brawl Leaves 1 Dead, Dozens Injured in UN Juba Camp," Radio Tamazuj (May 11, 2015), https://radiotamazuj.org /en/article/brawl-leaves-2-dead-dozens-injured-un-juba-camp.

4. United Nations Mission in the Republic of South Sudan, "Flash Human Rights Report on the Escalation of Fighting in Greater Upper Nile."

5. Human Rights Watch, *"They Burned It All": Destruction of Villages, Killings, and Sexual Violence in Unity State South Sudan* (July 22, 2015), https://www.hrw.org/report/2015/07/22/they-burned -it-all/destruction-villages-killings-and-sexual-violence-unity- state.

6. Ibid.

7. Ibid.

8. Hamilton, "Special Report: The Wonks Who Sold Washing- ton on South Sudan"; Leslie Goffe, "Hollywood's Role in South Sudan's Independence," BBC News (July 8, 2011), http://www .bbc.com/news/world-africa-14050504.

9. Hillary Rodham Clinton, "Press Availability with South Sudanese Foreign Minister Nhial Deng" (August 3, 2012), http://www.state .gov/secretary/20092013clinton/rm/2012/08/196050.htm.

10. John Tanza, "US Aid to South Sudan Exceeds $1 Billion," Voice

of America (April 23, 2015), http://www.voanews.com/content
/south-sudan-us-aid-billion/2732632.html.

11. Karin Zeitvogel, "US Aid to South Sudan Tops $1.3 Billion,"
Voice of America (September 23, 2015), http://www.voanews
.com/content/south-sudan-us-aid/2975657.html.

12. As of August 31, 2015, "the total cost of operations related to
ISIL since kinetic operations" started on August 8, 2014, is $3.87
bil- lion. Operation Inherent Resolve, Department of Defense,
http://www.defense.gov/News/Special-Reports/0814_Inherent
-Resolve.

13. "Statement by the National Security Advisor Susan E. Rice on the
South Sudan Peace Agreement" (August 26, 2015), https://
www.whitehouse.gov/the-press-office/2015/08/26/statement
-national-security-advisor-susan-e-rice-south-sudan-peace.

14. "Statement of President Barack Obama Recognition of the
Republic of South Sudan."

Index

About Nick Turse

Nick Turse is an investigative reporter, a fellow at the Nation Institute, and the managing editor of the Nation Institute's *TomDispatch.com*. He is the author, most recently, of *Tomorrow's Battlefield: U.S. Proxy Wars and Secret Ops in Africa* as well as the *New York Times* bestseller *Kill Anything That Moves: The Real American War in Vietnam*, which received a 2014 American Book Award. He is a contributing writer at the *Intercept* and has written for the *New York Times*, the *Los Angeles Times*, the *San Francisco Chronicle*, the *Nation*, and the *Village Voice*, among other print and online publications.

Turse has received a number of honors for his work including a Ridenhour Prize for Investigative Reporting, a James Aronson Award for Social Justice Journalism, and an I.F. Stone "Izzy" Award for Outstanding Achievement in Independent Journalism. Turse was awarded a Guggenheim Fellowship, a Lannan Foundation Writer's Residency in Marfa, Texas, and has previously been a fellow at Harvard University's Radcliffe Institute for Advanced Study and New York University's Center for the United States and the Cold War. He has a PhD in Sociomedical Sciences from Columbia University.

About TomDispatch

Tom Engelhardt launched *TomDispatch.com* in October 2001 as a private listserv offering commentary and collected articles from the world press. In December 2002, it gained its name, became a project of the Nation Institute, and went online as "a regular antidote to the mainstream media." Its mission is to connect some of the dots regularly left unconnected by the mainstream media and to offer a clearer sense of how this world of ours actually works.

Since its launch, *TomDispatch* has featured three original articles a week on a variety of topics from foreign policy to politics, with special focus on the U.S. military, the American empire, and other national security issues, as well as climate change and the environment. A mix of long-form essays, sharp commentary, and original reporting from around the world, *TomDispatch* serves as a newswire for scores of websites across the globe and is one of the most syndicated progressive websites in the United States.

TomDispatch regularly features Engelhardt's news analysis and commentaries as well as the work of authors ranging from Michael Klare, Andrew Bacevich, Laura Gottesdiener, Adam Hochschild, Noam Chomsky, and Nomi Prins to Rebecca Gordon, Alfred McCoy, Peter Van Buren, Ann Jones, Subhankar Banerjee, William Astore, Greg Grandin, and Karen Greenberg. Managing editor Nick Turse also regularly reports for the site on national security issues from the United States and overseas. Andy Kroll is *TomDispatch*'s associate editor and economic correspondent.

The late Jonathan Schell, who wrote regularly for the *New Yorker*, the *Nation*, and *TomDispatch* perhaps summed up the site best:

> At a time when the mainstream media leave out half of what the public needs to know, while at the same time purveying

oceans of official nonsense, the public needs an alternative source of news. Tom Engelhardt's *TomDispatch* has been that for me. With unerring touch, he finds the stories I need to read, prefacing them each day with introductions that in themselves form a witty, hugely enjoyable, brilliant running commentary on the times. He is my mainstream.

About Dispatch Books

While working at Pantheon Books in the 1970s and 1980s, Tom Engelhardt used to jokingly call himself publishing's "editor of last resort." His urge to rescue books and authors rejected or ignored elsewhere brought North America Eduardo Galeano's beautiful *Memory of Fire* trilogy and the world Art Spiegelman's Pulitzer Prize-winning *Maus*, among other notable, incendiary, and worthy works. In that spirit, he and award-winning journalist Nick Turse, author of the *New York Times* bestseller *Kill Anything That Moves*, founded Dispatch Books, a publishing effort offering a home to authors used to operating outside the mainstream.

With an eye for well-crafted essays, illuminating long-form investigative journalism, and compelling subjects given short shrift by far bigger publishing houses, Engelhardt and Turse seek to provide readers with electronic and print books of conspicuous quality offering unique perspectives on our disturbing planet. In a world in which publishing giants take ever fewer risks and style regularly trumps substance, Dispatch Books aims to be the informed reader's last refuge for uncommon voices, new perspectives, and provocative critiques.

Its first effort, *Terminator Planet*, explored how the military's increasing use of remotely piloted drones turned sci-fi visions of a dystopian future into an increasingly dystopian present. Since teaming up with Haymarket Books, one of the leading progressive publishers in the United States, Dispatch Books has put out Turse's *The Changing Face of Empire*, on the future of American warfare, and his investigations into shadowy U.S. military missions in Africa, *Tomorrow's Battlefield*. The imprint also scored a major success with Ann Jones's widely praised account of the human toll of the conflicts in Iraq and Afghanistan, *They Were Soldiers: How the Wounded Return from America's Wars: The Untold Story*. *Next Time They'll Come to Count the Dead: War and Survival in South Sudan* continues in this tradition of trenchant, shoe-leather reporting on distant wars and their painful aftermaths.

About Haymarket Books

Haymarket Books is a nonprofit, progressive book distributor and publisher, a project of the Center for Economic Research and Social Change. We believe that activists need to take ideas, history, and politics into the many struggles for social justice today. Learning the lessons of past victories, as well as defeats, can arm a new generation of fighters for a better world. As Karl Marx said, "The philosophers have merely interpreted the world; the point, however, is to change it."

We take inspiration and courage from our namesakes, the Haymarket Martyrs, who gave their lives fighting for a better world. Their 1886 struggle for the eight-hour day reminds workers around the world that ordinary people can organize and struggle for their own liberation.

For more information and to shop our complete catalog of titles, visit us online at www.haymarketbooks.org.

Also Available from Haymarket Books

The Changing Face of US Empire: Special Ops, Drones, Spies, Proxy Fighters, Secret Bases, and Cyber Warfare
Nick Turse

Tomorrow's Battlefield: US Proxy Wars and Secret Ops in Africa
Nick Turse

They Were Soldiers: How the Wounded Return from America's Wars—The Untold Story
Ann Jones